CAMBRIDGE SERIES ON HUMAN–COMPUTER INTERACTION

T0254420

The Reactive Keyboard

Cambridge Series on Human–Computer Interaction

The Reactive Keyboard

John J. Darragh
Department of Computer Science
University of Calgary, Alberta, Canada

Ian H. Witten
Department of Computer Science
University of Waikato, Hamilton, New Zealand

CAMBRIDGE
UNIVERSITY PRESS

CAMBRIDGE UNIVERSITY PRESS
Cambridge, New York, Melbourne, Madrid, Cape Town, Singapore,
São Paulo, Delhi, Dubai, Tokyo, Mexico City

Cambridge University Press
The Edinburgh Building, Cambridge CB2 8RU, UK

Published in the United States of America by Cambridge University Press, New York

www.cambridge.org
Information on this title: www.cambridge.org/9780521144766

First published 1992
First paperback printing 2010

A catalogue record for this publication is available from the British Library

Library of Congress Cataloguing in Publication data
Darragh, John J.
The reactive keyboard / John J. Darragh, Ian H. Witten.
    p.   cm. – (Cambridge series on human-computer interaction ;)
Includes bibliographical references (p.   ) and index.
ISBN 0-521-40375-8 (hc)
1. Human-computer interaction.   2. Electronic data processing – Keyboarding.
I. Witten, I. H. (Ian H.)   II. Title.   III. Series.
QA76.9.H45D37   1992   92-245
004'.01'9 – dc20   CIP

ISBN 978-0-521-40375-7 Hardback
ISBN 978-0-521-14476-6 Paperback

Contents

Figures and tables

Figures

Tables

Acknowledgments

We would like to acknowledge the enthusiastic support of David Hill, who motivated and nurtured our interest in human–computer interface design and has always taken a very active interest in special interfaces for disabled people. We are grateful to Michael Saya, Jim McLaughlin, the late Linda Barr, and the rest of the friendly and helpful staff at Calgary's Technical Resource Centre for introducing us to the technical aids literature; to John Arnott, Randy Jones, Peter Nelson, Alan Newell, and Gregg Vanderheiden for their inspiring comments and discussions; and to Tim Bell and John Cleary for their help with the text compression aspects of the work. Bill McGarry, the moderator of the "misc.handicapped" newsgroup on USENET, kindly sent us information on several commercial packages for predictive text input.

The various implementations of the Reactive Keyboard would not have been possible without a great deal of help from our friends. The UNIX version owes much to Dan Freedman, who created the input line editor; Doug Taylor, who added command and file completion; and Jason Penney, who cleaned up large parts of the code. The code was ported to the IBM PC by Dejan Mitrovic, and further refined, documented, and packaged by Donna Choquette. The Macintosh interface was created by Mark James. We would also like to acknowledge Richard Esau, Radford Neal, and Ron Newman for their various programming efforts. Tim Bell carefully read the manuscript and provided many useful suggestions. Tamara Lee did a marvelous job of patiently and tirelessly redrawing the figures.

Without a lot of encouragement from friends and acquaintances we would surely never have completed this book. Harold Thimbleby was the one who actually suggested that we write it. We have been spurred on by positive feedback from users of the Reactive Keyboard, particularly from the USENET community. Saul Greenberg has been a continual source of enthusiastic support for this work. Finally, and above all, a special thank you to our families – Alfred, Anna, Anne, Brian, Joan, Marina, Nikki, Pam, and Scott – who helped us in so many ways during the course of this work.

This research has been supported by the Natural Sciences and Engineering Research Council of Canada, the Alberta Heritage Foundation for Medical Research, the University of Calgary's Special Projects Fund, and Esso Resources Canada Ltd.

PART I

Communication disability and predictive text generation

1
Communication and communication aids

If all my possessions were taken from me with one exception, I would choose to keep the power of communication, for by it I would soon regain all the rest.
— *Daniel Webster*

The ability to communicate is so fundamentally human that most of us take it completely for granted. Having learned to speak, gesture, and write, people take little notice of the cognitive and physical complexity of these behaviors. We are accustomed to the speed and flexibility offered by a variety of natural communication modes. It is only when our communication abilities are hampered that we are forced to take notice.

Sudden loss of communication ability can be devastating. One clear summer's day in 1978, during a first ascent of an unclimbed peak in the Monashee mountains of British Columbia, one of the authors (JJD) was struck by falling rock that broke his back. Following a seven-hour wait while his companions sought help, a second rockfall occurred while he was on a stretcher, breaking his neck. Following this near-fatal accident, he was temporarily paralyzed and unable to speak due to a tracheotomy. The only way he could communicate was through eye movements. His sister wrote the alphabet on a large sheet of cardboard and proceeded by pointing to letters that she predicted would come next in his communication. These were accepted by vertical eye movements, and rejected by horizontal ones. Communication, although laborious, was surprisingly rapid, particularly for expressing basic needs that could to some extent be anticipated in the limited context of an intensive care unit.

Eye movements alone provide an unusual and frustratingly slow communication channel, which can nevertheless be effective – indeed almost indispensable – if other communication modes are unavailable. There are many ways that people can express and receive information. As Figure 1.1 illustrates, it is usually transmitted through facial expressions, gestures, speech, touch, and written symbols; and received through senses of hearing, touch, and sight. Associated with each communication mode is a normal rate of expression or comprehension – for instance, adult conversational speech rates range from 126 to 172 words per minute (wpm). Communication rates are rarely noticed when they are normal. However, communication may falter and break down altogether if these rates are somehow greatly reduced.

Unfortunately, extremely slow communication is a daily reality for some people. Rate of expression is significantly reduced by several forms of physical disability,

3

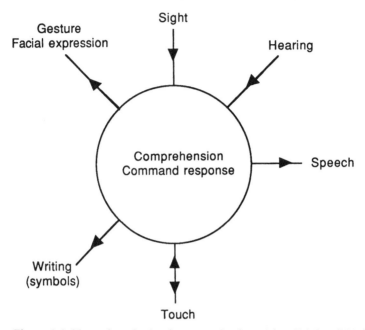

Figure 1.1. Normal methods of communication. After Shipley (1980).

and for those afflicted, unaided spoken and written communication may be intolerably slow – even nonexistent. In order for such individuals to participate effectively in society a means of facilitating and accelerating their rate of expressive communication has to be found. This is achieved by the use of "communication aids" – devices that augment the ability of a physically disabled person to converse.

The experience of severe loss of communication, and the clear advantage of human-mediated prediction in accelerating information transfer, motivated us to consider how existing communication aids could be improved by incorporating predictive techniques. We have developed a device called the Reactive Keyboard that accelerates typewritten communication with a computer system by predicting what the user is going to type next. Obviously predictions are not always correct, but they are correct often enough to form the basis of a useful communication device. Because predictions are created adaptively, based on what the user has already typed in this session or in previous ones, the system conforms to whatever kind of text is being entered.

To give a foretaste of what it is like to use the Reactive Keyboard, consider how helpful it would have been to Thomas Hardy when writing his novel *Far from the Madding Crowd.* It begins:

When Farmer Oak smiled, the corners of his mouth spread till they were within an unimportant distance of his ears, his eyes were reduced to chinks, and diverging wrinkles appeared round them, extending upon his countenance like the rays in a rudimentary sketch of the rising sun.

Of course, little of this would be predicted if the Reactive Keyboard started out unprimed, with no prior experience of English. More representative of the usual situation is the typing of, say, the last sentence of the first chapter once the Reactive Keyboard had seen the preceding text. This goes:

Gabriel, perhaps a little piqued by the comely traveller's
indifference, glanced back to where he had witnessed her
performance over the hedge, and said, "Vanity."

Having typed the first letter, the system predicts that it will continue "abriel Oak as he." The first word can be taken from this prediction with just one selection operation – whether a single keystroke or a mouse click, depending on the version of the Reactive Keyboard being used. Hardy's next two letters, a comma followed by a space, are presented as one of predictions that will follow "Gabriel"; thus they can be accepted as a single unit. The next word, "perhaps," has not appeared before in Chapter 1 of the novel; neither have "piqued" or "comely." Consequently the Reactive Keyboard gives little help with these words, although sometimes two letters can be entered together. Once the "a" of "traveller" has been entered, the completion "velling out of doors" is predicted and the first four letters can be selected. After the first few letters of "indifference," the remainder of the word is predicted, as is "glanced" once its first few letters are entered.

Table 1.1 illustrates the entry of the second line of the above quotation. To the left is the growing line of text, and to the right the progression of predictions from which the text is selected. Each line corresponds to just one selection, taking the first few letters of the prediction and appending them to the line so far. In reality, all the action takes place on a single line of the display, with alternative predictions in a separate window. There are 27 lines in the table (excluding the last one), indicating that 27 selections are needed to enter the whole line of text, which contains 57 letters – thus, on average, just over two letters are entered per selection. The Reactive Keyboard not only helps to complete words, but can also predict phrases. For example, once the first part of "witnessed" is entered, the remainder is predicted along with the "her" that follows and the spaces that flank it. This prediction is based on an earlier appearance of "possessed her" in the first chapter. The predicted strings do not necessarily appear in Hardy's text: For example, the prediction "[in]dulge in such a leafless seaso[n]" in the second line of the table is an amalgam of "indulge in such a performance" and "at such a leafless season"; and "to test her hat" (at the end of the eleventh line) derives from "to test her capacity" and "adjust her hat"!

In sum, out of the 164 letters (including punctuation and spaces) that make up Hardy's sentence, nearly half are predicted by the system as the most likely one to follow. The remainder are presented on a menu of alternative predictions, and Hardy would have had to scan down this menu to find the appropriate text. However, the predictions are presented in order of likelihood and so it is not

Table 1.1. *Predicting a line of* Far from the Madding Crowd

Line so far	Prediction
	in•which•had•clothed•it•in•the
in	dulge•in•such•a•leafless•seaso
ind	ing•into•the•idle•deed•a•novel
indi	fference•was•irresistible•by•G
indifference	,•and•painted•a•soft•lustre•up
indifference,•	generous•though•he•fain•would
indifference,•g	lass.•She•did•not•intrinsicall
indifference,•gla	nced•over•him,•and•the•whole•c
indifference,•glanced•	between•the•waggon•had•been•he
indifference,•glanced•b	able•triumphs• — •the•smile•beg
indifference,•glanced•ba	ctitious•one,•to•test•her•hat,
indifference,•glanced•bac	ket•she•wore,•and•painted•a•so
indifference,•glanced•back	•hair.•The•myrtles,•geraniums,
indifference,•glanced•back•	them;•more•probable•triumphs• —
indifference,•glanced•back•t	o•the•idle•deed•a•novelty•it•d
indifference,•glanced•back•to•	were•alone•its•spectators,• —
indifference,•glanced•back•to•w	hole•concern•of•horses,•waggon
indifference,•glanced•back•to•wh	ether•the•smile•began•as•a•fac
indifference,•glanced•back•to•whe	re•the•object•of•his•contempla
indifference,•glanced•back•to•where•	heard•returning.•She•put•the•g
indifference,•glanced•back•to•where•he	•had•lost•her•hat,•or•pat•her
indifference,•glanced•back•to•where•he•had•	won.•Still,•this•was•but•conje
indifference,•glanced•back•to•where•he•had•w	ith•a•peculiar•vernal•charm.•W
indifference,•glanced•back•to•where•he•had•wit	n•the•fresh•and•green,•and•at
indifference,•glanced•back•to•where•he•had•witn	e•thing•to•signify•that•art,•)
indifference,•glanced•back•to•where•he•had•witne	ss•of•an•originality.•A•cynical
indifference,•glanced•back•to•where•he•had•witness	ed•her•to•indulge•in•such•a•
indifference,•glanced•back•to•where•he•had•witnessed•her•	point,•and•we•know•how•

usually necessary to scan far before finding the desired letter. For example, in the first line of the table, the prediction "in•which•had•clothed•it•in•the" is the ninth item on the menu of alternatives, and its first two characters, "in," are selected. The desired prediction generally appears in the first dozen or so, and on average Hardy's chosen letter occurs at the beginning of the seventh prediction.

As well as assisting with the entry of free text, the Reactive Keyboard has proved even more useful in enhancing the command interface to operating systems by predicting commands, arguments, and filenames. It has been used regularly for some time by physically disabled university students as their standard command interface to the UNIX operating system. Their combined daily experience amounts to approximately six years. One types with a single partially paralyzed hand and uses the system for entering commands and electronic mail. He estimates that over a two-year period it has provided assistance on over 30,000 host system commands, averaging 10 predicted characters per command, and writes:

The Reactive Keyboard has dramatically changed the way I use computers. I now use much longer, more descriptive, filenames than I otherwise would have without its reliable recall and typing assistance. I also rely completely on the Reactive Keyboard to remember such things as electronic mail addresses and long complex command-line sequences. Life online would just not be the same without it.

The Reactive Keyboard has recently been released on an international computer network, and the following comment is typical of those received:

I have cerebral palsy, so my typing is a little bit impaired. I am very impressed with your program. It seems to be ideal for significantly speeding up my typing in the shell while I am programming. I like it a lot, and it saves me a lot of time. I am very glad to have it available to me.

The Reactive Keyboard is just a program – it does not require any special equipment, other than a suitable computer. Figure 1.2 shows it in operation. Versions exist for various different computer systems. The program can be used in conjunction with a variety of input devices – for example, mice, conventional keyboards, and specialized aids such as the single-handed keyboard that can be seen in Figure 1.2.

This book describes the background to the Reactive Keyboard, and the technical and human interface techniques used in its design. It contains complete details of the system, including the full program source code that you can type in from Appendix B. The program is available free, and is provided in source form to encourage people to modify it for particular purposes and disabilities. It can be obtained electronically over Internet (see Chapter 7 for details).

This book is divided into two parts. Part I, comprising Chapters 1, 2, and 3, covers background material – the functional architecture of a communication aid, the idea of predictive text generation systems, the important distinction between adaptive and nonadaptive models, and precursors to the Reactive Keyboard system. Part II, comprising Chapters 4, 5, and 6, discusses the system itself: its user interface, design, and implementation. The "predictive" component of the system, which forms the kernel of the device, is separated from its "user interface." The predictive technique is presented in detail and a program is given that implements

Figure 1.2. Using the Reactive Keyboard.

it, written in the C programming language. In general, user interfaces can be tailored to both situation and disability, and three existing interfaces are described.

This chapter sets the scene by introducing communication disability in general and the enhancement of expression rate in particular, by examining the architecture of communication aids, and by providing an analytical framework for describing communication aid fluency. It closes with a discussion of communication task modeling.

1.1. Communication disability

Many physical disabilities can adversely affect a person's expressive communication ability, including traumatic head or spinal cord injury, cerebral vascular accident or "stroke," amyotrophic lateral sclerosis (ALS or Lou Gehrig's disease), congenital defects, and various neuromuscular diseases such as cerebral palsy and multiple sclerosis. Very little quantitative information is available on the number of people suffering from particular communication disorders, although it has been estimated that over a million people in the United States alone are both mute and physically impaired. Regardless of the actual numbers involved, few would disagree that society must do all it can to help these people communicate.

Table 1.2. *Typical rates of manual expression*

Mode	Rate (words per minute)	Reference
Inexperienced typing	10.2	Chapanis et al. (1972)
	18	Weeks et al. (1974)
Experienced typing	18.1	Chapanis et al. (1972)
	27	Weeks et al. (1974)
Handwriting	23.5	Seibel (1972)
Single-switch scan	≤1 to 5	Rosen & Goodenough-Trepagnier (1982a)
	0.5 to 3	Kelso & Vanderheiden (1982)

Individuals with expressive communication disabilities can be grouped into two broad categories: (1) those who are incapable of speech and (2) those who lack the physical ability to write. People frequently fit into both categories, because disabilities that impair speech often compromise physical strength and dexterity as well. In either case, an alternative means of expression must be provided in the form of a manually operated speech or writing aid. These are collectively called "expressive" communication aids, distinguishing them from devices such as hearing aids and magnifying glasses that are intended to enhance sensory perception. Potential users of expressive aids have conditions that affect speech and/or writing ability but leave language, reading, and some motor skills intact.

Expressive communication aids may find application for able-bodied people as well. The proliferation of public information terminals creates a demand for interfaces that allow limited command and text input, and that are extremely robust and tamper-proof. Low-bandwidth graphical input devices, such as trackballs or touch-screens, can be used together with predictive text generation techniques for incidental text input.

The speed with which one can transfer information is critical, and the demand for reasonable speed is extremely high. Normal rates of manual expression appear to have an upper limit imposed by the physical dynamics of the neuromotor system. The upper part of Table 1.2 summarizes the results of experiments on normal expressive communication rates using various means, in words per minute. Typical values for expressive typing and handwriting are 15 wpm for inexperienced but able-bodied typists, around 25 wpm for experienced typists, and again about 25 wpm for handwriting.

The expressive writing rates of nonvocal communication aid users, however, are usually much lower. Severely disabled people use communication aids operated by a single switch that is to be closed when a scanning light reaches the correct letter.

Figure 1.3. Single-switch communication aids: linear scan (top) and matrix scan (bottom).

These can be arranged in configurations such as the linear and matrix devices depicted in Figure 1.3, as will be discussed in more detail later. The lower part of Table 1.2 shows the results of experiments with users of such aids: rates of 1 wpm or less are typical, and rates of more than 5 wpm are rare.

Expressive rates of 0.5 to 3 wpm are particularly distressing when speech is absent and writing is the only means of conversing. It has been demonstrated that 3 wpm is the *absolute minimum* rate tolerable for interactive conversation. At less than 9 wpm, impatience of the receiver is strongly inversely proportional to rate.

1.2. Enhancing expression rate

In nonvocal communication systems, faster is better. Designers seek ways to boost the low communication rate of people with severe physical disability. A great variety of aids have been devised, ranging from simple letterboards, where users spell words they are unable to speak by pointing at letters on a board, to sophisticated microcomputer-based aids linked to speech synthesizers, where users press buttons labeled with predefined words and phrases that are then synthetically spoken for them. The advent of inexpensive microcomputers has led to a proliferation of new and dynamic "high-tech" aids. However, even with the sophistication of many of the newer aids, users continue to be faced with the problem of slow information transfer in interaction and writing.

A typical communication aid user has severely limited physical strength and endurance, and it becomes necessary to *amplify* and *accelerate* each physical movement or input stroke they make. Amplification increases the productivity of each stroke, for example by entering several letters at once through abbreviation expansion. Acceleration decreases the time taken for an input stroke by making likely elements easier to select. A wide variety of amplification and acceleration techniques can be used to speed up communication aids.

Selection sets

Selection sets contain visual building blocks that can be used to compose messages. They can be constructed because language is redundant. Selection sets are compiled by extracting frequently used language fragments from samples of representative target communication, of a genre the user is expected to generate. They typically include a variety of elements, such as letters, words, phrases, or even ideas in iconic form. Messages are composed by concatenating selected language elements together. A sentence could be composed, for example, by selecting an appropriate sequence of predefined words and phrases.

Most communication aids offer their users a predefined set of fixed size. A trade-off is made between communication speed, or "fluency," and available selection set vocabulary, or "articulateness." Greater rate enhancement is possible if the set contains elements closely matched to the user's personal communication patterns, because more productive, and hence fewer and faster, selections can be made. Conversely, if a fixed set is used for different communication needs, discrepancies will arise between desired messages and the samples from which the selection set was derived. This necessarily compromises both fluency and articulateness. To attain maximum rate enhancement, more personalized selection sets must be used.

Adaptive predictive strategy

With predefined selection sets, as the size of the set is increased articulateness grows, but fluency tends to decrease. *Adaptive* selection sets provide a potent means of avoiding the negative consequences of this trade-off. By adjusting automatically to the individual user's characteristic language patterns, they are capable of removing the vocabulary constraint imposed by predefined sets without adversely affecting fluency. Personalized selection sets are constructed progressively by continually monitoring and remembering user-selected language element *sequences*. Later, these stored concatenations can be offered for selection as though they were single elements: one selection replaces many. Because fewer selection strokes and correspondingly less time and effort are required to generate messages, the physical burden on the user decreases and communication rate increases.

The continuous monitoring inherent in adaptive systems can be further exploited by associating and storing a *context* with each concatenation. Predictions of highly likely future selections – in other words, continuations – can be made at each choice point by recalling concatenations that the user generated in similar contexts in the past. A subset of highly probable continuations can then be preferentially offered to the user for selection, ensuring rapid access to the most significant parts of the evolving selection set. The potential benefits of this adaptive predictive strategy have led to the concept of the Reactive Keyboard, a context-sensitive adaptive predictive text generation system suited to the writing needs of many people with expressive communication disabilities.

1.3. Components of a communication aid

Communication aids can be defined as devices that augment the ability of a communicatively handicapped person to produce communication signals. There are nearly as many different kinds of communication aids as there are communication disorders. Because of this diversity, several different functional breakdowns of communication aid components have been suggested. The one depicted in Figure 1.4 provides a good general foundation.

Four separate functional components are shown: the *input device, output devices, selection algorithm,* and *prompting device.* The first, which might be a joystick or pneumatic switch, translates the user's physical movements into input signals. The second, typically a typewriter page, cathode ray tube (CRT) display, or speech synthesizer, displays the selected symbol or symbols. More than one output device may be available through a single communication aid. The selection algorithm generates a group of candidate symbols and uses the input signal to select one from it. The prompting device, which may be a CRT display or a cycling light, reminds users what symbols are currently available for selection and informs them of the actions required to make a selection. Simple examples of the latter are the linear scan and matrix scan devices (see Figure 1.3).

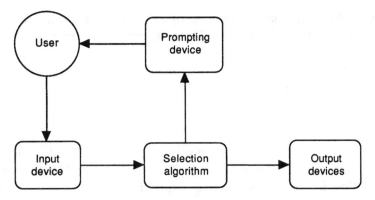

Figure 1.4. Components of a communication aid.

Input device

An ever-increasing array of special-purpose and adapted input devices are available to the communication aid user. The importance of the input device in the success of a communication aid cannot be overemphasized. Individuals must be carefully matched with appropriate input devices in order to ensure maximum benefit, and the greatest possible element selection speed can be gained through having the most appropriate input device for a user. The protocol for input device evaluation and selection, well known by communication therapists, is a matter of assessing residual physical ability. However, the details of input device selection are beyond the scope of this book.

The large variety of input devices can be divided roughly into two main groups: *discrete* (digital) and *proportional* (analog). The first comprises mechanical and electromechanical switches and groups of switches. The most basic kind of discrete device is the on/off switch: Examples are a single switch and a puff-and-suck pneumatic switch. More control is provided by four-position joysticks and multi-button keypads. The second group includes devices that produce variable or encoded position-dependent signals, for example analog joysticks and mice.

Proportional input devices make it possible to access large arrays of characters almost as rapidly as small ones. Though long neglected as input devices for communication aids, they are now being used in some systems – including the Reactive Keyboard. While the limitations of traditional discrete controls force users to adopt stepwise sequential or encoded access, analog controls allow them to point directly to displayed options. With a proportional-controlled positioning system, a selection can be indicated very rapidly by skipping quickly to the immediate vicinity of the target, then slowing down and zeroing in on it. However, there are some disabled people who find proportional input devices difficult to use. Systems that rely exclusively on such devices create new barriers for them.

The rate-enhancing potential of analog input devices has stimulated the development of many unusual input devices. These include light-beam pointers, where a head-mounted light beam is used to select language elements from a video display, and eye-position detectors, where the direction of gaze is used to select those elements that the user looks at.

Output device

A communication aid's output device displays user-selected symbols or language elements. Three broad classes of device can be identified, based on the longevity of the information display: permanent (e.g., typewriter page), temporary (e.g., CRT display), and transient (e.g., speech synthesizer). The most suitable type depends on each particular user's communication needs and environment. Clearly, output devices must operate in a medium appropriate to all potential receivers of the message. Communication aid speed is normally independent of the output device used. There has been a trend over the past few years toward "high-tech" transient and temporary output devices. However, it is still important that nonvocal people are provided with the ability to communicate in writing, in order that they may realize more of their potential to contribute to today's society.

Selection algorithm

Using a limited number of switches to select a rather large number of language elements requires some method of mapping or encoding of language elements into a sequence of input device switch closures. This is the function of the selection algorithm of Figure 1.4. Three methods are in common use: *scanning, encoding,* and *direct selection* – the one chosen depends on the number of switches that the user can repeatedly and reliably activate. Progressing from scanning to encoding to direct selection, the number of switches increases and the complexity of the selection algorithm decreases correspondingly.

Figure 1.5 gives the three possibilities. In *scanning,* the communication aid steps through a series of options and the user responds with a single switch when the desired item is reached. To speed input, letters can be presented so that more likely ones are offered first. This is achieved by ordering them in their frequency of occurrence in English, namely "etaoin sdhrlu." With *encoding,* the user enters elements of a memorized code on a limited keypad or input device to recall previously stored language fragments. *Direct selection* employs a pointing device to select items from a prompting device. The pointing device might be a bank of switches, in which case there is a one-to-one correspondence between switch closures and selected symbols, as on a typewriter keyboard.

Element selection speed is one of the most important considerations in communication aid design. Each language element is encoded as a sequence of strokes, where a stroke is defined as the motor activity that causes an input signal. A

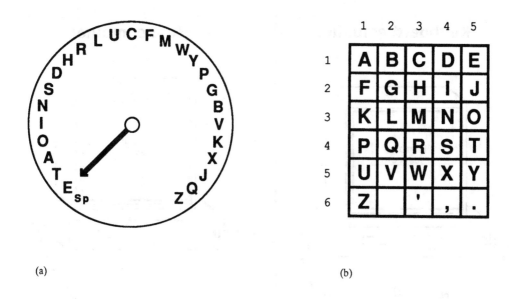

(a)

(b)

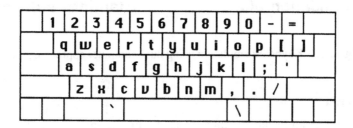

(c)

Figure 1.5. Common selection algorithms: (a) scanning, (b) encoding, and (c) direct selection.

selection algorithm's speed is directly related to the efficiency with which the set of possible input signals is encoded into the selection set of possible language elements. Direct selection is the swiftest method, whereas scanning is the slowest. Scanning is often machine-paced and limited by inter-item step time, whereas with encoding and direct selection the user may become faster with practice. Fast, efficient selection algorithms are essential for achieving maximum fluency.

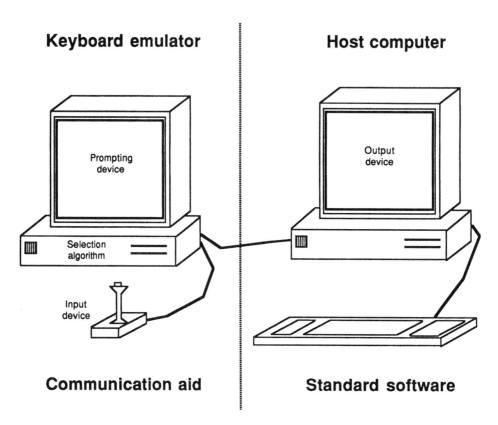

Keyboard emulator   **Host computer**

Prompting
device

Output
device

Selection
algorithm

Input
device

Communication aid   **Standard software**

Figure 1.6. Keyboard emulation using dual-computer approach.

Prompting device

The final communication aid component is the prompting device. It displays a
visual representation of the communication aid's underlying selection algorithm
and encoding scheme, thereby providing the user with a visual model of the
operation of the aid. The design of the prompting device must take account of the
user's visual acuity and scanning idiosyncrasies, and provide a clear, uncluttered
display with meaningful visual feedback.

An example: the keyboard emulator

The fluency of use of a communication aid is dictated by the success of the match
between the user and the four components: input device, output device, selection
algorithm, and prompting device. If two or more of these components can be
combined, the chain of events involved in generating input is shortened and
communication may be hastened. Most communication aids combine their selection algorithm and prompting device in a single unit. A particularly relevant
example is a class of aids known as *keyboard emulators*.

Keyboard emulators are communication aids that interface transparently to a separate host computer system by mimicking the computer's input signals. Input from the emulator appears to the host computer to be coming from its regular keyboard rather than from a special communication aid. People with expressive communication disabilities interact with standard software running on the host computer through input devices attached to the keyboard emulator and specialized software that runs on it. This allows them to use standard, unmodified software packages such as text editors, spreadsheets, and databases, through an interface that is tailored specifically to their disability. The keyboard emulator concept has been referred to by a variety of names such as *electronic keyboard, surrogate keyboard,* and *visual keyboard.* Most emulators are themselves microcomputer based, giving rise to the dual-computer approach to communication aid design as shown in Figure 1.6. The four communication-aid components are identified in the diagram.

1.4. Communication fluency

Optimizing the fluency of nonvocal communication through fine tuning of selection rate and productivity is a challenging problem. In contrast with technological developments for the implementation of communication aids, there has been little progress toward a *science* of nonvocal communication.

Rate factors

A large number of interacting elements contribute to communication fluency: the attributes of individual users, general human factors, and various features of the communication aid itself. Also important are environmental issues such as the mode of the communication – whether it is real-time conversation or composing playback messages for later use. User-specific attributes include residual communication abilities, movement and reaction times, physical and mental endurance, and experience and motivation – all largely beyond the control of aid designers. Substantial rate enhancements can be achieved by concentrating on general human factors design principles and aid-specific components.

Design guidelines that take into account various human factors are well known to human–computer interface designers, but have only recently been applied to communication aid design. Elements such as cognitive load, physical load, and visual load are important in the design of effective systems.

Aid-specific factors that influence communication fluency directly include the appropriateness of the input device for the user, the selection algorithm, the prompting device display, the system's learnability and internal consistency, its error rate and error recovery scheme, the acceleration and amplification techniques employed, spelling assistance, the degree of explicit personalization available, usability of the aid, and the degree of user satisfaction. Features that affect selection rate and selection productivity are the most important.

Table 1.3. *Typical nonvocal communication rates*

Value	Units	Reference
3.4 to 5.7	selections/minute	Clarkson & Poon (1982)
1.6 to 4.9	selections/word	Goodenough-Trepagnier et al. (1982a)
0.5 to 3.0	words/minute	Kelso & Vanderheiden (1982)

The newness and complexity of microprocessor-based aids has led to a proliferation of divergent approaches. Different researchers have adopted different criteria for measuring the rate of communication, and Table 1.3 shows some typical nonvocal communication rates. Notice how low the wpm range is when compared to that of able-bodied people shown in Table 1.2 – well under the minimum 9 wpm that receivers feel comfortable with in an interactive situation. The rates are reported in different units, namely *average selection rate* in selections per time, or inversely time per selection, average *selection productivity* in selections per word, or words per selection, and average *overall fluency* expressed as words per time. These units are related, and we next introduce some notation that allows their relationship to be expressed clearly.

An analytical framework

A good analytical framework should permit the characterization of systems that are diverse in detail of execution, in a way that emphasizes the generic similarities among them. We proceed first by defining a simple set of system descriptors, then go on to demonstrate their relation to communication rates, and finally use them to highlight trade-offs inherent in the design parameters of communication aids.

Three interdependent system variables of time, length, and cost are defined:

time T is the average time to perform a motor act (time/stroke)

length L is the average number of strokes per selection (strokes/selection)

cost C is the average number of selections per word (selections/word)

The average time to form a word is

$$t = T \times L \times C \text{ (time/word)}$$

Applying these definitions to the units in Table 1.2, the average selection rate is $1/TL$ (selections/time), selection productivity is $1/C$ (words/selection), and the overall fluency is $1/t$ (time/word).

The goal of a communication aid is to optimize each variable, minimizing t to maximize fluency. The form of the fluency equation $t = T \times L \times C$ reflects a natural division of the design factors into those determined by the input device (T), the selection algorithm (L), and the selection set (C). The time T reflects user-specific motor control capability as measured by the selection stroke time imposed by a particular input device and disability. The length L characterizes the selection algorithm that maps sequences of interface acts – for example, switch closures – on to the selection set. The cost C is a function of the composition of the selection set, and may be viewed as an inverse measure of efficiency.

Two independent system variables are useful for discussing the design trade-offs implicit in the fluency equation:

> number N is the number of elements in a selection set
>
> buttons B is the number of distinct inputs, or "buttons," in the interface

For direct selection these are equal: $N = B$, which means that L is 1. For encoding, N is greater than B and L is greater than 1.

The size N of the selection set has a direct effect on the average number of strokes L needed to access an element. Selection productivity, $1/C$, grows with N because larger selection sets can contain longer, more productive elements. Therefore, associated with increasing selection set size is a fluency trade-off between cost C and length L. Increasing N raises L while simultaneously lowering C. There is evidence in practical communication aids that a reduction in C more than counterbalances the increase in code length required for encoding the larger system. This means that lower cost in selections per word – in other words, high selection productivity – is desirable even at the expense of adding steps to access additional elements.

There is also a fluency trade-off between time T and average number of strokes per selection L that depends on B, the number of distinct inputs available. Increasing B raises the average stroke time T – this is called "Fitts' Law" – and lowers L, with competing effects on t that resemble the cost/length trade-off just discussed. It has been reported that fluency is improved using more buttons, in spite of an increase in T. This means that a greater number of distinct inputs is desirable even at the expense of higher stroke time.

Acceleration and amplification

The techniques used to increase selection rate $1/TL$ (selections/time) and selection productivity $1/C$ (words/selection) are known as *input acceleration* and *input amplification* respectively. Table 1.4 lists a variety of acceleration and amplification techniques.

Acceleration seeks to decrease T and L by improving the input device or selection algorithm to make language elements faster and easier to select. Possible

Table 1.4. *Input acceleration and amplification techniques*

Input acceleration	
Improved input device	
1. Increasing the number of input switches in encoding or scanning	Goodenough-Trepagnier et al. (1982b)
2. Using proportional input for direct selection[a]	Gaddis (1982), Rosen & Goodenough-Trepagnier (1982a)
Improved selection algorithm	
3. Increasing single-switch scan dimensionality	Rosen & Goodenough-Trepagnier (1982b)
4. Sorting selection elements in decreasing frequency order	Baletsa et al. (1976), Thomas (1980)
5. Dynamically sorting selection elements by frequency[a]	Jones (1981), Witten et al. (1983)
6. Adapting selection sets to current context	Baletsa et al. (1976), Pickering & Stevens (1984), Thomas (1980)
7. Dynamically adapting selection sets to current context[a]	Witten et al. (1983)
8. Using hierarchical presentation	Buhr & Holte (1981), Vanderheiden (1983)
Input amplification	
1. Using abbreviation expansion	Kelso & Vanderheiden (1982), Vanderheiden (1983, 1984), Young (1981)
2. Using partially automatic word completion[a]	Witten et al. (1982, 1983), Pickering & Stevens (1984)
3. Presenting longer language elements	Brady et al. (1982), Vanderheiden (1983)
4. Presenting concatenated language elements[a]	Witten et al. (1982, 1983)

[a]Indicates techniques used in the Reactive Keyboard.

methods include increasing the number of input switches in encoding or scanning, using proportional input for direct selection, increasing single switch scan dimensionality, sorting selection elements in decreasing frequency order, adapting selection sets to the current context, and using hierarchical presentation.

Amplification attempts to improve productivity by decreasing the cost of each selection, namely C (selections/word). Possible methods include using abbreviation expansions, using partially automatic word completion, presenting longer language elements, and presenting concatenated language elements. Acceleration and amplification techniques are often used together.

1.5. Communication models

Every communication aid incorporates a model of the communication task it is designed to facilitate. Models include a set of language elements from which the user can choose (the selection set) and a technique for making choices (the selection algorithm).

Techniques for user modeling in interactive computing can be classified according to whether they place the burden of modeling on the designer, the user, or the machine. Four classes can be identified:

canonical modeling, where the designer of the system models the user

explicit modeling, where users model themselves

automatic modeling, where the system models the user

combination modeling, which fuses the automatic and explicit methods

Although originally developed to describe interactive computer interfaces, this taxonomy is general enough to pertain to the problem of communication aid design – after all, modern communication aids are almost exclusively based on interactive microcomputer systems. Each kind of modeling technique has advantages and disadvantages. The boundaries between the four classes are somewhat blurred, and a well-designed system will likely use combinations of different modeling techniques to present the best adaptive system.

Canonical models

Modeling is *canonical* when the designer provides a language model for the user. This is both straightforward in concept and easy to implement. Its main disadvantage is lack of flexibility. Such systems often constrain their users by a less than perfect, nonadaptive, largely inefficient language model. Canonical models are constructed based on designer intuition, analysis of user needs, analysis of user vocabulary and usage, or – preferably – by involving the user directly in the design process. The final communication model design is frozen and cannot be adapted to suit different users' needs, or the changing needs of one user over time.

Explicit models

Modeling is *explicit* when users themselves are able to provide a limited model of characteristics and/or actions that the system is to follow in particular situations. Any actions that users take to adjust the system to better suit themselves become part of the model. Models are constructed jointly by the designer, who provides facilities for system personalization, and individual users, who explicitly tailor the system to their needs. Explicit models are more effective than canonical ones because they can be personalized – at least to some extent. However, they suffer from the disadvantage that the user must learn to set them up and maintain them. In practice, people often use default settings, a practice that in effect reverts to a canonical model. Moreover, the subsystems created to facilitate the user's construction or modification of a model may be complex in their own right, possibly negating any benefits. The time and effort required to create an explicit model distracts, albeit temporarily, from the task the communication aid is intended to perform.

Models are *consulted* when the facilities that they provide are invoked. Explicitly constructed models may be consulted explicitly by the user or implicitly by the system. An example of the former is user-defined abbreviations, which must be accurately recalled in order to be used. An example of the latter is a "set-up" profile, which automatically executes a list of commands when the system is started up.

Automatic models

Modeling is *automatic* when the system models the user. Like explicit modeling it has two distinct stages, model construction and model consultation. Construction differs from explicit model construction in that the system uses limited cues and rules to guess likely user behaviors. An automatically constructed model is generally probabilistic, and any given prediction may be inaccurate – particularly if it incorporates user errors as though they were part of the user's intended behavior.

Most automatic systems construct their models from scratch by continuously monitoring user behavior patterns and updating internal user models to reflect changing behavior. A generally less satisfactory alternative is for the system to infer what type of user it is dealing with and automatically select a suitable model from a range of user stereotypes and associated default models. This approach is not seen in communication aid designs because it is very difficult to deduce the user's experience level automatically – though this has been attempted in experimental computer systems. The first approach, involving continuous monitoring and model updating, is used extensively in the Reactive Keyboard and to a limited extent in other predictive text generation systems.

Models formed automatically are consulted either partially or totally automatically. Both techniques result in an action visible to the user. They offer different degrees of user control over system-initiated actions. As the name implies, totally automatic consultation performs a visible action – like moving a cursor – without user intervention. Partially automatic consultation might suggest an action, but query the user for acknowledgment before performing it. Either way, serious problems can arise when an action is performed at an inappropriate time, for the user may develop a negative view of the system. Rigorous checks and balances in model modification and elicitation are necessary for a system to appear consistent and sensible to the user.

Combination models

The final form of user modeling is really just a mixture of automatic construction and explicit model consultation techniques. A fusion of the best aspects of each method is achieved by removing the tenuous and perhaps rather artificial boundaries between them. The user effort required to construct an explicit model is absent as the model is automatically constructed and inappropriate system action is avoided because the model is explicitly consulted. (Partially automatic consultation achieves the same effect.) In combination modeling, issues such as user control, model accuracy, and the user's perception of the system will determine the relative weight of explicit and automatic techniques in the composite system.

1.6. Further reading

A comprehensive discussion of manual expression rate for people who lack speech is given by Foulds (1980), including the typical communication rates for able-bodied people that are quoted in the first part of Table 1.2. References giving communication rates for disabled people are cited in Tables 1.2, 1.3, and 2.1. Figure 1.1 is adapted from Shipley (1980), which appears in a useful collection of papers on the use of technology in the care of the elderly and disabled. The estimate of 126 to 172 wpm for normal adult conversational speech rates is from Perkins (1971). The single-handed keyboard that can be seen in Figure 1.2 is manufactured by P.C.D. Maltron Ltd. Figure 4.2 shows a close-up view.

Goodenough-Trepagnier and her co-workers have made numerous contributions to the study of interfaces for the disabled. For example, Goodenough-Trepagnier et al. (1984) discuss minimum tolerable communication rates for interactive communication. The analytical framework introduced in this chapter is developed by Goodenough-Trepagnier and Rosen (1982) and Goodenough-Trepagnier et al. (1982b). Fitts' Law was introduced by Fitts (1954).

Vanderheiden's group at the University of Wisconsin–Madison has also contributed widely to the field, including an early review of nonvocal communication techniques (Raitzer et al., 1976) and a particularly relevant recent survey of fixed-vocabulary communication acceleration techniques (Vanderheiden and Kelso, 1987). He was one of the first to recognize the potential of microcomputers in the design and implementation of communication aids (Vanderheiden, 1981).

Vanderheiden also inspired the dual-computer approach in Figure 1.6 (Vanderheiden, 1982; Vanderheiden and Kelso, 1982). This is one way of implementing keyboard emulators (Kelso and Gunderson, 1984; Rogers et al., 1982), which have been referred to variously as "electronic keyboards" (Henle, 1981), "surrogate keyboards" (Brown et al., 1982), and "visual keyboards" (Shein, 1988a, 1988b). The "emulating interface" is a recent development in keyboard emulators that mediates between the user's communication aid and both keyboard and mouse controls of the host computer system. An example is T-TAM, the "Trace transparent access module" (Schauer et al., 1990), which accepts inputs from standard communication aids and produces signals for an IBM PS/2 or Apple Macintosh computer. It is available from the Prentke Romich Co. (see Appendix D).

References to various acceleration and amplification techniques are cited in Table 1.4. The functional architecture of Figure 1.4 and Section 1.3 is due to Buhr and Holte (1981). Many other communication aid structures have been described in the literature, for example by Morasso et al. (1979), Ring (1980), and Shein et al. (1989). Various selection algorithms are also described by Damper (1984). Gaddis (1982) demonstrated the suitability of proportional input devices for enhancing expressive communication rate. An interesting example is the head-mounted pointing device originally developed by Gunderson et al. (1982). However, as Brownlow et al. (1990) and Shein et al. (in press) point out, a system whose operation depends on proportional input devices such as mice can create new barriers for disabled people who find them difficult to use. Several alternatives to direct graphical selection have recently been suggested as possible solutions (Hamann, 1990; Pon and Tam, 1990; and Shein et al., 1990). Chizinsky (1990) describes a number of readily available keyboard interfaces that enable users to access Apple Macintosh computers without having to use a pointing device.

Two good general introductory books to computer-based aids for disabled people are Lindsey (1987) and Pressman (1987). Comprehensive information on input devices for the disabled is given by Vanderheiden and Grilley (1976), Charbonneau (1982), Staisey et al. (1982), Durie (1983), and in a recent book by Lee and Thomas (1990). An excellent four-volume book describing specific devices has been compiled by Brandenburg and Vanderheiden (1987), while another useful and comprehensive source is ABLEDATA (Hall et al., 1989). These resources are available on CD-ROM (as well as in printed form) from the Trace Research and Development Center (see Appendix D). Further information on personal computer devices for the disabled can be found in "IBM Special Education Resources," available from the National Support Center for Persons with Disabilities (see Appendix D); and "Apple Computer Resources in Special Education and Rehabilitation," available from DLM Teaching Resources (see Appendix D).

The four classes of user model were identified and described by Greenberg (1984, 1988). The question of deducing the user's experience level automatically is addressed by Rich (1983).

2

Predictive text generation systems

Research on predictive text generation was triggered in the early 1970s by the observation that some people were using letter, word, and phrase predictions to accelerate communication with totally paralyzed individuals. When expressive communication can take place only at the rate of a word or two per minute, there is very strong motivation for the listener to take active steps to increase the rate. In practice, able-bodied listeners spontaneously begin to try to accelerate conversation using a suggestion-and-acknowledgment strategy.

This works as follows. Anticipating the next word or phrase to be communicated, the receiver points to likely next letters on a letterboard, or suggests a likely word or phrase completion. The paralyzed person responds using distinctive eye movements to accept or reject the receiver's predictions. It is clear that accurate predictions can greatly enhance the paralyzed person's expressive communication fluency, for a single letter or two is often a sufficient cue for the receiver to guess a word, and two or three words in a sentence are often all that is needed to guess an entire sentence accurately. By proceeding in this fashion, it is possible to communicate at a rate that is several times faster than that at which the person would normally be able to communicate.

The ability to guess or predict next letters or words relies on the statistical redundancy of language. In the late 1940s Claude Shannon, the father of information theory, estimated that English is about 75% redundant. He noted that, in general, good prediction does not require knowledge of more than a fairly small number of preceding letters of text. While for a native speaker success in predicting English gradually improves with increasing knowledge of the past, apart from some statistical fluctuation, it does not improve substantially beyond knowledge of 8 to 10 preceding letters.

Communication aid designers reasoned that if all n-letter sequences or "n-grams" present in a suitably large text sample or word list were tabulated, the result, known as an n-gram table, might then be used to make predictions of likely next letters or words. Knowing a user's first $n - 1$ letter selections would make it possible to predict likely n'th letters by retrieving items that begin with this prefix. In order to decrease the average selection time, more likely predictions could be offered to the user first. Alternatively, predictions could be made by using word prefixes to retrieve likely completions from dictionaries of frequently used words.

Work began in the mid-1970s to determine whether a simple n-gram letter anticipation technique, built into a microcomputer-based communication aid, could provide communicatively disabled people with a more efficient means of expression. The first predictive text generator, called ANTIC, was investigated around

Table 2.1. *Early predictive text generation systems*

System	Buttons	n-gram length	Communication rate (words per minute)	Reference
TIC (nonpredictive)	1	1	5	Baletsa et al. (1976)
ANTIC (predictive)	1	4	6.8 to 7.8	Baletsa (1977)
MCCS (predictive)	2	2	6.0 to 7.5	Gibler (1981)

1974 at Tufts University, Boston, and later, in 1980, the MCCS system was introduced at Northwestern University, Chicago. It is interesting to compare these systems with a nonpredictive predecessor called TIC, Tufts Interactive Communicator, which used an 8 × 7 scan matrix that was sorted in letter-frequency order – hence TIC effectively used an n-gram length of one. Table 2.1 reproduces experimental results for the three systems and shows that both predictive systems were capable of faster communication rates than the nonpredictive one, although the experiments used very few subjects.

The creation and evolution of predictive text generation systems have closely followed advances in microcomputer technology. Initially, the rather small memory and limited computational resources of microprocessors constrained the designer. As improved microcomputers became available, the potential for enhancing the simple n-gram letter anticipation techniques used in ANTIC and MCCS grew to the point where it became a realistic proposition to equip a system with more sophisticated predictive capabilities.

2.1. Predictive text generation

Predictive text generation is a context-sensitive technique for enhancing expressive communication rate. The idea is to suggest what the user might want to type next, on the basis of preceding input. Information about the context and frequency of past selection set accesses is exploited to predict future selections. Likely continuations are identified by locating a *context* of recent selections (of length, say, $n - 1$ letters) in a large memory of previously encountered element sequences (n-gram tables or equivalent). Frequency-of-occurrence data are then used to sort predictions and offer them to the user for selection, in decreasing order of probability – thereby both accelerating and amplifying user inputs.

Predictive vs. nonpredictive systems

Predictive systems differ from their nonpredictive counterparts primarily in the way they deal with message composition. Figures 2.1 and 2.2 show the difference

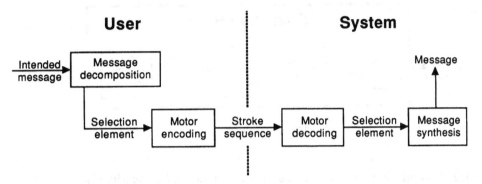

Figure 2.1. Nonpredictive message composition. Based on Rosen and Goodenough-Trepagnier (1982a).

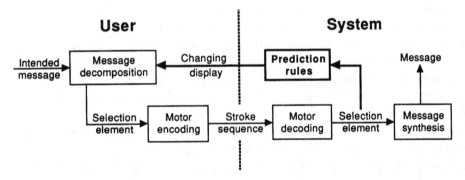

Figure 2.2. Predictive message composition. Based on Rosen and Goodenough-Trepagnier (1982a).

diagrammatically. In both cases, users *decompose* their *intended message* into a series of *selection elements* (references to components of the figures are italicized). Each element is then selected using a *sequence of input strokes*. Finally, the system *synthesizes* the series of *selection elements* back into the user's intended *message*. The difference between predictive and nonpredictive systems lies in the selection elements that are offered to the user. Nonpredictive ones (Figure 2.1) present users with a fixed set of selection elements that are equally accessible at each choice point. Predictive systems (Figure 2.2) use *prediction rules* to make likely elements easier, faster, and more productive to select.

Figure 2.3 shows some common features of predictive systems by expanding on the *prediction rules* of Figure 2.2. Progressing from right to left, the system monitors user selections (*selection elements*) and stores the last few together in *short-term memory* to form a *current context*. This context is sought in *long-term memory* to find likely *continuation elements* and associated probabilities of occur-

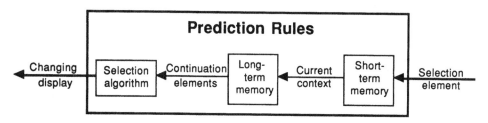

Figure 2.3. The predictive component.

rence. This information is processed by the system's *selection algorithm* to generate a *changing display* of the selection set on the aid's prompting device.

Adaptive vs. nonadaptive models

Every communication aid incorporates a model of the communication task it is designed to facilitate. Models include the language elements the user can choose (the selection set) and the technique for making selections (the selection algorithm). Many aids embody static models, created by the designer for all users and frozen for the lifetime of the device. For example, a predictive system could be designed to use a fixed set of common words and phrases thought to be representative of a typical user's input.

Alternatively the model could be dynamic, adapting to its user's vocabulary and phrasing. *Adaptive* systems employ models that are based on what the user has already entered – both in this session and, perhaps, in previous ones too. This is an example of an automatic modeling technique (see Section 1.5 in the preceding chapter). Adaptive models automatically adjust themselves to individual user idiosyncrasies and are therefore generally superior to canonical models. Canonically defined models are giving way to more personalizable adaptive models in an effort to win further increases in communication rate.

Long-term memory

Predictive text generation systems form their predictions by consulting long-term memory. This contains a large number of recurring selection element sequences (n-grams), with associated occurrence frequencies. The current context, $n - 1$ most recent selections stored in short-term memory, is used to look up likely continuations. In other words, predictions are made on the basis of the present situation, represented by short-term memory, and past experience, represented by long-term memory. The prompting device display normally changes after each user selection to present a new subset of predicted elements, in probability order. A four-phase cycle of *user selection, short-term memory update, long-term memory lookup,* and *display update* continues for the duration of a message composition session. When adaptive modeling is used, long-term memory is also updated.

Several types of communication model and memory structure are possible based on the various levels of redundancy present in natural language. Language redundancies range from lexical, through to syntactic, semantic, and even pragmatic levels. Such models span the disciplines of computational linguistics and artificial intelligence and become increasingly difficult to generate and utilize at the higher levels. In this book we consider only n-gram-based orthographic models. These have been used in most predictive text generation systems to date and are particularly suitable for adaptive techniques. They are constructed canonically from representative text samples, and automatically by monitoring the user's text generating behavior letter by letter.

A model's predictive power depends on how accurately its experience matches the user's current communication needs, and on the length (n) and number of stored sequences. Better predictions are possible when long-term memory is large and n is close to Shannon's recommended 8 to 10 characters. Unfortunately, the storage space required to tabulate n-grams increases exponentially with their length, and this imposes practical upper bounds on the value of n.

Matching predictive text generation to the user

For two decades the dictum "know the user" has been a fundamental guiding principle in interface design. The designer should be intimately acquainted with the user's needs, experience, and the conditions under which the task will be performed. He or she should be familiar with the user's particular situation, and understand the limitations, strengths, skills, and characteristics of humans in general.

An assessment of residual communication function is the first step in evaluating a disabled client for a communication aid. Potential users can be identified by looking at the physical and cognitive attributes they need in order to benefit from predictive systems. Table 2.2 groups communication functions into three classes: those essential to use such systems, those that must be at least partially intact, and nonessential attributes. Because of the highly visual orientation of predictive text generation, it is not surprising that visual acuity, language skills, and reading skills are essential. Perhaps more surprising is the fact that full cognitive function is *not* essential. Indeed, a so-called "brain prosthesis" (*sic*), which has been developed for aphasic brain-damaged people, uses a predictive word completion strategy (ISP/1, described in Section 2.3).

Most users of text generation systems lack one or more nonessential functions. Individuals with severe physical disabilities that impair speech, limb function, and manual dexterity are obvious candidates – their need triggered research on predictive text generation systems in the first place. People with very low or nonexistent hearing acuity also stand to benefit. Their need to attain a reasonable telephone conversation rate has led to the incorporation of predictive elements into a speech-to-text/text-to-speech telephone communication system.

Table 2.2. *Residual communication function requirements*

Requirement	Residual functions
Essential	Visual acuity
	Language skill
	Reading skill
Partial	Cognitive function
Nonessential	Speech
	Limb functions
	Manual dexterity
	Hearing acuity

Source: Based on a table in Shipley (1980).

2.2. Does prediction help?

The pros and cons of using prediction in a communication aid are outlined in Table 2.3. The principal advantages include communication rate enhancement, reduced physical load, reduced cognitive spelling load, and increased articulateness. Rate enhancement is achieved using acceleration and amplification techniques to make the selection of likely language elements faster and more productive. The result is that both the average number of strokes per selection (i.e., "length" as defined in Chapter 1) and the average number of selections per word (i.e., "cost") approach one. Note that cost values may be less than one, if whole phrases are predicted. Physical load on the user is reduced as fluency increases – less time and effort need be expended to generate a message. Spelling errors are reduced by offering most likely letters first, providing a strong visual cue to correct spelling, or predicting correctly spelled word or phrase completions, which forestalls misspelling altogether. Finally, the context- and frequency-sensitivity of predictive systems allows rapid access to very large and rich selection sets. The net result is a faster, easier to use, more productive communication aid.

However, predictive techniques have a number of potential disadvantages, as will be discussed.

Unlearnability

With practice, communication aid users invariably become faster at using their aids. Because predictive aids adapt constantly to the user's vocabulary and language usage, they are inherently unlearnable, and this may reduce the potential for rate increase with practice. Moreover, the prompting display may change dramati-

Table 2.3. *Advantages and disadvantages of predictive text generation*

Known advantages
Rate enhancements through acceleration and amplification
Reduced physical load on the user
Reduced cognitive spelling load: forestalling misspelling
Fast access to large, rich, personalized selection sets

Possible disadvantages
Essentially unlearnable (as are all) systems with large memories
Visually demanding, requiring constant visual vigilance
May interrupt the user and force him to respond before continuing

cally at each choice point. Large memories and constantly changing prompting displays make predictive systems potentially confusing and difficult to learn; this may distract from the primary communication task.

However, the slow reaction and movement times of a typical user constitute the rate-limiting factors, and they swamp unlearnability as a serious concern. Considering the clinically demonstrated rate improvements, presented in Table 2.1, for the ANTIC and MCCS systems, which use simple canonical predictive models, the potential rate loss due to unlearnability seems insignificant.

Visual vigilance

A related but more serious concern is the visual demand that predictive text generation systems inevitably place on their users. Considerable vigilance is required. Users must constantly direct their attention to the prompting device in order to evaluate the predictions that are offered. However, these systems were originally designed in an attempt to accelerate the extremely low communication rate achieved by users of one- or two-switch scanning aids, where visual monitoring of a prompting device display is the standard operating strategy. The use of a predictive technique probably makes little further demand on the user's attention. Predictive text generation systems succeed where a visual selection strategy such as display-based scanning or direct selection is appropriate.

Visual workspace allocation is a major challenge faced by system designers. Display space must be divided between the prompting device and the message composition area. Menus of selection elements may consume most of an aid's display space, restricting that available for message composition. This issue is often addressed by using two separate displays, one for the aid's prompting device and the other for message composition (see Figure 1.6). However, visual discontinuity arises if attention is simultaneously demanded by two separate displays. These workspace limitations are now being partially overcome with the introduction of larger multiwindowed systems where one physical device includes both logical displays.

Dialog determination

A final possible disadvantage relates to the degree of control the user has over the system. It has been suggested that word prediction is undesirable in that it forces the user to respond to the aid. However, this confuses prediction per se (which is good) with overdetermined model consultation (which is bad). Dialog determination, a measure of how well dialog control is shared between the system and the user, is an important consideration in any user interface – and doubly so in adaptive systems. Too little determination of the dialog by the system and the user gets confused, too much and they feel confined and the dialog seems forced. A careful balance must be struck. Predictive text generation systems demand thoughtful user interface designs that avoid overdetermination and automatic mode changes.

2.3. Predictive text generation systems

We now survey some existing predictive text generation systems to provide a basis for comparing and evaluating alternative system designs. They fall into three general categories: letter anticipators, predictive word or phrase completors, and combined systems that use both letter anticipation and predictive word completion.

Letter anticipators

The first predictive systems, ANTIC and MCCS, date from the late 1970s. They are simple letter anticipators that accelerate input by making likely next letters faster and easier to select. They are both based on a row-column selection algorithm, where the system steps through a letter matrix, highlighting one row at a time. Both use an n-gram based prediction technique to speed up selection. However, they differ considerably in the way they derive and employ their respective n-gram models. Similarities and differences are given in Table 2.4.

The TIC system

Tufts Interactive Communicator (TIC) was the predecessor of ANTIC, and although it is not a predictive system it will be described first to put ANTIC in context. It is a single-switch row-column scanning aid based on the 8 × 7 letter matrix shown in Figure 2.4a. The system illuminates successive rows of letters at a predetermined speed that can be adjusted by the user. When the row containing the desired element is reached, the user activates an input switch, at which point the system begins scanning across the columns, highlighting individual entries. When the desired row-column item is reached, a second switch closure selects it.

The dependence of selection time on matrix position is shown in Figure 2.4b. The numbers represent how many machine-paced delays are needed for each character. For example, to type the "space" character (the blank cell at the top left) the user first closes the switch to select the first row, and then closes it again immediately to select the first column. Thus no machine-paced delays need elapse,

Table 2.4. *Key features of three scanning letter anticipators*

Feature	MCCS	ANTIC	DM
Buttons B	2	1	1
Elements N	30	56	30
Stroke reduction	14%	30%	56%
Model type	Canonical	Canonical	Automatic
Model order (n)	2	4 (partial)	1 to word-length
Model source	Newman's text	Newman's text	User inputs
Source size	250,000 chars	250,000 chars	4,500 words
Model size	8 Kbytes	4 Kbytes	8 Kbytes
Microcomputer	Motorola 6800	RCA 1802	Aim-65
Reference	Heckathorne et al. (1980)	Baletsa (1977), Thomas (1981)	Jones (1981), Myers (1982)

although there will be an inevitable neuromotor delay in switch closure. As another example, the letter L will require four machine-paced delays. At first the first row is illuminated and one delay must elapse before the machine reaches the second row. Then the user immediately closes the switch and scanning begins along that row. Another three delays must elapse before it reaches the fourth column, whereupon the switch is immediately closed to select the L.

The matrix is arranged according to the frequency of letters in English. The most commonly occurring character is space, and thereafter the most frequent letters are E, T, A, O, I, N, . . . , in that sequence. These are assigned to the cells of Figure 2.4a in the order of increasing delay according to Figure 2.4b.

The ANTIC system

Anticipatory TIC (ANTIC) extends TIC by using prediction to offer sequentially up to two likely letters before commencing the row-column scanning described already. These two initial predictions are illuminated in turn. If either is correct, a single input switch closure will select it, preempting row-column scanning for that character.

Predictions are based on a static model and do not adapt to the user's inputs. The model is formed using quadgram statistics (model order of 4, as noted in Table 2.4), which includes interword spaces so that prediction across word boundaries is possible. Because only two predictions are displayed following any particular context, not all quadgrams need to be stored. Moreover, in order to economize

(a)

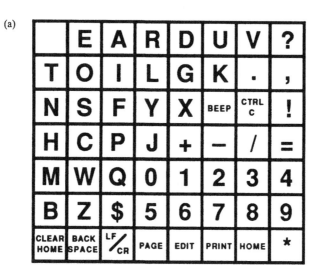

(b)

0	1	2	3	4	5	6	7
1	2	3	4	5	6	7	8
2	3	4	5	6	7	8	9
3	4	5	6	7	8	9	10
4	5	6	7	8	9	10	11
5	6	7	8	9	10	11	12
6	7	8	9	10	11	12	13

Figure 2.4. The TIC communication aid: (a) letter matrix and (b) scan delay for each matrix element. Adapted from Demasco and Foulds (1982).

further on space, some of the less frequent combinations are omitted. These stratagems reduce the total quadgram storage requirement to four Kbytes.

The system's developers examined three types of scan matrix layout to determine the most effective display format: *fully dynamic, partially dynamic,* and *static.* The first layout presents a new probability-ordered matrix layout after each letter selection. The second uses six dynamical elements in the upper left corner of an otherwise static letter matrix. The third displays a fixed, unchanging matrix. The fully dynamic scanning matrix was deemed unsuitable because the continually changing display would require great vigilance on the part of the user. Early experiments suggested that a fully dynamic keyboard requires so much concentration and contributes to so many errors that this would not be a desirable method to use. Later work with a partially dynamic version was abandoned when a subject complained of being confused by the lights flashing before his eyes. A static display prefixed by up to two linearly scanned predictions was found to be least distracting and confusing to the user.

This system demonstrated the feasibility of using n-gram based predictions to speed up a scanning communication aid. A speed increase of 33%, along with a 30% reduction in input strokes, was realized over TIC. ANTIC's designers pioneered the use of n-grams derived from large samples of representative text. They also demonstrated that fully dynamic or partially dynamic displays are unsuitable when the scanning rate is determined by the machine, as is usually the case in single-switch devices. They later upgraded their system to include words and phrases in its scan matrix by using a three-dimensional scanning selection algorithm that allowed the user to choose between several different scanning matrices. The new system, called QUICKTIC, employs the same letter anticipation technique as ANTIC.

The MCCS system

TIC and ANTIC are one-switch, machine-paced, aids. The Micro-computer Communication and Control System, or MCCS, was the first two-switch scanning aid to incorporate letter anticipation. Its prompting device is implemented on a 24-line by 40-column video display. The scanning matrix is fully dynamic, and scanning speed is under user control, only one row being presented at a time. If the desired element is not in that row, a special element is selected to display the next scanning row. When the row containing the desired element is located, one switch is used to advance the cursor to highlight the element, and the other switch is activated to select it.

MCCS uses an order-2, or "bigram," model for prediction (Table 2.4). However, its model does not incorporate the space character. As a consequence, a "floating" space is included in the scan row, moving closer to the first scan position as more letters of a word are selected. The space character initially follows five letters in the matrix row. With each letter selection, it is shifted one position toward the beginning of the group, making it successively easier to select .

Whereas ANTIC was specifically designed as a nonvocal speech prosthesis, MCCS was intended as a writing aid for severely disabled people. It proved slower than ANTIC despite the use of full bigram tables and two input switches. The

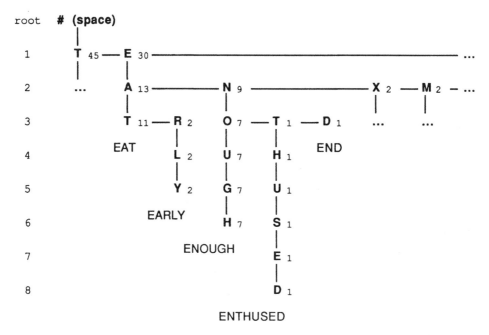

Figure 2.5. Dynamic Matrix (DM) sorted binary tree structure. Derived from Jones (1981).

difference probably lies in their respective model orders – in other words, n-gram lengths – and prediction presentation schemes.

The DM system

A more recent one-switch letter anticipator, the Dynamic Matrix, or DM, is similar to the (rejected) fully dynamic version of ANTIC, having a 5 × 6 rather than an 8 × 7 letter matrix. Its n-gram model differs considerably from those of ANTIC and MCCS in three respects: source; order, that is, value of *n;* and structure.

DM was the first predictive system to derive its n-gram model adaptively from the user's own letter selection patterns. It accomplished this by building an internal binary search tree (Figure 2.5) that is updated with each letter selected. The space character forms the root of the tree. This is followed by frequency-ordered lists of letters found in the first and subsequent letter positions of words – levels one through eight in Figure 2.5. Each entry in a given list shares a common word prefix that can be reconstructed by searching through levels from the root. A frequency-ordered list of letters most likely to follow a given prefix is found at the next level of the tree. Each entry, in effect, points to a frequency-ordered subtree of possible continuations or suffixes.

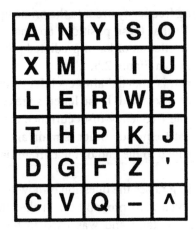

Figure 2.6. Dynamic Matrix (DM) following entry of #E.
Derived from Jones (1981).

For example, suppose the letters "space" and E have been selected. A list of likely letters can be found by tracing the space/E context from the top of the sample tree structure in Figure 2.5. Space is the root, and E is the second entry at level one, which in turn points to a level-two list of likely letters starting with A, N, X, and M.

Each letter entry contains a frequency-of-occurrence count to permit sorting and subsequent optimization of the scan matrix. The frequency count of an entry with no suffix subtree represents the total number of times a particular word has been encountered. In effect the tree stores all the words that the user has entered, in a structure that facilitates letter prediction. Figure 2.5 contains five examples of words starting with EA and EN. The sequence #EA, for instance, has been seen a total of 13 times: 11 times in the word #EAT, and twice in the word #EARLY (where "#" is used to represent the space character).

The letters entered so far constitute a word prefix that is used as a variable-length n-gram context for prediction. The context length grows with each letter selection, and more refined predictions are made until "space" is selected. As each letter is selected, the newly lengthened word prefix is used to locate a context-specific list of likely next letters in the tree structure. The list is then used to generate a new scanning matrix, making the most likely letters faster to select by positioning them in the upper left corner of the scan matrix. When space is selected once again, the context length is truncated to one, retaining the space alone, and a matrix of most likely first letters is again offered to the user, based on level one in Figure 2.5.

Figure 2.6 shows a scan matrix generated from the sample tree in Figure 2.5 after the characters # (space) and E have been selected. The letters A, N, X, and M are most likely to follow #E in the next letter position, as can be seen from level two in

Figure 2.5. They are assigned in descending frequency order to the prime upper left matrix positions. (Recall from Figure 2.4b that these positions are the fastest to select.) The other matrix positions are also filled in order of predicted probability, although the full prediction tree is not shown in Figure 2.5.

The tree-structured model is adaptive and is updated after each letter selection. One of two actions will occur when a letter is selected. If the letter is present in the tree, the tree is updated by incrementing the frequency-of-occurrence counter for that letter, and then re-sorted to ensure that frequency order is maintained. If the letter is not yet present, the new letter is added to the end of the current list with a count of one.

DM's use of automatic adaptive modeling raises the question of how to arrange letters in the matrix that have equal or even zero probability. In the first case, alphabetical order seems to be a sensible default and was used in the MCCS system. Another alternative is to present them in recency order, where the most recently selected elements are displayed first. The zero-probability case is an example of the "zero-frequency problem" in which probability estimates must draw on some knowledge of the problem itself. In this case, it seems reasonable to rank characters that have not yet occurred in order of their frequency in ordinary English text.

Memory limits and ongoing automatic modeling introduce a new feature: selective memory, or "forgetting." DM uses a word sequence counter to indicate when a word was last used. When memory is full, less valuable words are removed to make room for new ones being entered.

DM's main contributions to the design of predictive text generation systems are the use of adaptive modeling and forgetting, the use of a variable-length context, and the use of a flexible tree-structured n-gram data store.

Detailed comparison of these three letter anticipators is difficult because their user interfaces are so different. If we look solely at the reported input stroke reductions listed in Table 2.4, a general trend emerges: Input stroke savings tend to increase with both the order and the completeness of the n-gram model used, as expected. They will also increase with the goodness of fit between the model source and the user's intended genre of text.

These early letter anticipators teach some important lessons in system design. First, as shown by the improved performance of ANTIC over TIC, n-gram based prediction is capable of substantially lowering the average number of strokes per selection, that is, the length L. Second, as shown by the improved performance of DM over ANTIC, adaptive, user-derived, automatic models appear to greatly surpass canonical models in terms of reduced values of L. Third, if a good interface design is used, this reduced L is reflected in increased fluency. Fourth, fully dynamic prediction display is not appropriate when the interaction is machine-paced. Fifth, incomplete higher-order models outperform complete lower-order models. Sixth, automatic modeling raises entirely new issues, such as forgetting,

Table 2.5. *Key features of four predictive word completors*

Feature	MAC	MOD	PAL	ISP/1
Buttons B	1+	1+ or proportional	1	1 or proportional or keyboard
Elements N	500	500	1,000	7,000
Stroke reduction	1+	1+	1+	2 or 3
Model type	Canonical	Automatic	Automatic	Canonical/ explicit
Model consultation	Explicit	Partially automatic	Partially automatic	Partially automatic
Presentation	Alphabetic	Recency	Frequency/ alphabetic	Recency/ frequency
Word display	One page	10 or 20	10	(a) 5 to 10 (b) up to 26
System type	Stand-alone writing aid	Keyboard emulator	Stand-alone writing aid	Stand-alone speech aid
Reference	Clarkson & Poon (1982)	Nelson et al. (1984)	Arnott et al. (1984)	Colby (1984)

the zero-frequency problem, and the question of correcting mistakes such as spelling errors in automatically constructed models.

Word completors

The need to increase the productivity of user selections has led to the development of a second kind of system: input-amplifying predictive word completors. Word completors augment letter-by-letter spelling schemes by adding dictionaries of frequently used words. Dictionary words are displayed selectively, based on a context of one or more initial letters, and accepting a predicted word completes the initial user-spelled word prefix. Considerable savings in the average number of strokes per selection (i.e., cost C) accrue if long words are predicted and selected after only one or two prefix letters are chosen. Exploiting word-prefix context to progressively refine the word list that is offered can also yield considerable savings in the average number of strokes per selection (i.e., length L), by making more likely words quicker to select.

Four microcomputer-based predictive word completors, MAC, MOD, PAL, and ISP/1, are listed in Table 2.5. MAC, Mac-Apple Communicator, was developed at

King's College, London; MOD, originally for Mouth-Operated Dynamic keyboard, at the National Research Council of Canada, Ottawa; PAL, Predictive Adaptive Lexicon, at the University of Dundee in Scotland; and ISP, Intelligent Speech Prosthesis, at the University of California School of Medicine, Los Angeles. These systems have dictionaries of 500 or more words in addition to single letters, punctuation, numbers, and control elements. They can all operate in a single-switch scanning mode. MAC and MOD can exploit multiple switches, while MOD and ISP/1 can utilize proportional inputs. Only ISP/1 can accommodate a full QWERTY keyboard. All are implemented on commercially available microcomputer systems and use standard video displays as prompting devices.

These systems differ largely in the way they construct and consult their word dictionaries. MAC and ISP/1 have predefined dictionaries of frequently used words, derived from unspecified sources. ISP/1 goes beyond MAC by allowing the dictionary to be modified explicitly to include commonly used phrases and alternative spellings – this is particularly useful since it is a speech aid for brain-injured people. MOD and PAL derive their word dictionaries automatically from spelled user inputs. New words, not previously in the dictionary, are added as they are spelled. If the dictionary becomes full, one or more least recently (MOD) or least frequently (PAL) used words are deleted to make room for a new word. MOD has the additional feature that undesired words can be deleted explicitly, and automatic modeling can be turned off and the dictionary frozen in its current state: This is reported to assist with dictionary construction for those who find dynamic construction unnerving.

MAC is the only system that insists on explicit model consultation. After one or more letters are selected, the user has the option of completing the spelling or else switching to a word completion dictionary. A major drawback of this strategy is that users must remember what words are in the dictionary in order to decide which option to choose.

MOD, PAL, and ISP/1 employ partially automatic word list consultation; this is much easier to use than explicit consultation. The first two systems display context-specific (i.e., word-prefix-specific) lists of 10 or 20 likely words after one or more initial letters have been selected. The original scanning matrix remains visible and active, providing visual continuity and allowing for continued letter selection and concomitant word list refinement without any explicit user action. When a desired word is displayed it can be selected and the prefix completed without further spelling. After a word is selected, a list of most frequently used words, unconditioned by any context information, is shown.

ISP/1 operates in a similar way, but does not display word lists until two or three letters are selected, at which point the display switches to a list of up to 36 words or phrases. Most word lists appear after two-letter selections. However, when the bigrams CO, IN, PR, or RE are selected a third character is required because these prefixes are so common that word lists conditioned on the bigrams alone would overflow a single display page.

The last major difference between these systems lies in the order in which predicted completions are shown. MAC takes the simplest, though least effective, approach of offering word completions alphabetically. The other three systems rearrange presentation order based on recency of use (MOD), frequency of use (PAL), or both (ISP/1). MOD uses a simple push-down stack dictionary structure where new words are added to the top of the dictionary list. If the dictionary is full, the least recently used words are simply dropped off the bottom when new ones are added. Reused words are deleted from their old position in the stack, and then treated as if they were new. PAL presents word lists based on frequency of access. The 10 most frequently used words are presented in alphabetical order. Least frequently used words are simply deleted when new ones are added to a full dictionary. ISP/1 presents two double-column word lists. The upper list contains the 5 to 10 most recently used words, labeled by digits. The rest of the display is filled with up to 26 remaining words or expressions in frequency order, labeled by letters.

Both MOD and PAL derive their word lists adaptively from user inputs, necessitating mechanisms to avoid the incorporation of spelling errors. MOD saves newly spelled words in a temporary holding buffer until the next word is entered. If an error is noticed in a word before the next one is completed, it can be corrected using editing commands. A facility for deleting unwanted words from the dictionary is also provided.

Quantitative benefits arising from using word completion dictionaries, in terms of average number of strokes per selection (length L) and average number of selections per word (cost C), are not reported for any of the systems.

These word-completion systems augment the lessons learned from earlier letter anticipators. First, partially automatic model consultation appears to be superior to explicit consultation. Second, automatic word list derivation is desirable, and again leads to the concepts of forgetting and error correction. Third, large numbers of words and expressions can be accessed rapidly using this technique. Fourth, the display order for the word list can be alphabetical, recency-based, frequency-based, or some combination of these, and may have an adaptive modeling component.

Combined systems

Word completion strategies form a natural extension to letter anticipation schemes. Indeed, one letter anticipator, MCCS, has been modified by the addition of word completion dictionaries, resulting in the combined CDC (Communication and Device Control) system. This retains the original letter anticipation spelling scheme but switches to word completion if a known two-letter word prefix is entered. It then behaves like the word completors discussed in the previous section by offering a list of likely word completions to the user for selection.

Table 2.6. *Key features of the CDC system*

Feature	Letter anticipation	Core dictionary	Learning dictionary
Elements N	30	500	100
Model type	Canonical	Canonical	Automatic
Model order (n)	2	2	2
Model source	Newman's text	Word list	The user
Source size	250,000 chars	1 million words	User sessions
Buttons B	2		
Stroke reduction	5% (relative to ANTIC)		
Microcomputer	Apple II, 48 Kbytes RAM, 1 disk drive		
Model size	Less than 48 Kbytes		
Reference	Heckathorne & Childress (1982, 1983)		

Features of CDC are summarized in Table 2.6. Its word dictionary has two parts: a canonical 500-word core derived from the most frequently used words in the Brown Corpus, a standard corpus of American English text, and a user-derived automatic learning dictionary storing up to 100 words. After two initial letters have been selected using the letter anticipation scheme, both dictionaries are searched for possible completions. Any that are found are automatically displayed in a frequency-ordered list, six words at a time. Core elements are displayed before any learning elements. If the desired word is located and selected, it is added to the growing text buffer; otherwise letter-by-letter anticipatory spelling is resumed and the newly spelled word is added to the learning dictionary. Once the 100-word learning dictionary is full, new words replace the oldest and least frequently used ones in order to keep the dictionary current and topical.

No rate enhancement analysis has been published for CDC in a 500/100 dictionary configuration, though reference is made to extensive research on a 1000/200 dictionary configuration. The larger dictionaries apparently led to a 24% drop from 3.88 to 2.95 input strokes per letter over the otherwise identical nondictionary MCCS system. Unfortunately, only a 3% to 10% overall fluency enhancement was achieved. This figure rose to 30% if all the words were in the dictionaries, yielding an overall communication rate of approximately 10 words per minute. Even with the larger dictionaries, CDC's complete bigram-based scheme improves on ANTIC's partial quadgram letter anticipation by only 5%. This may be because higher-order models, larger and more personalized dictionaries, and more effective user interface designs are necessary if significant communication rate enhancements are to be realized.

2.4. Recent predictive interfaces

In recent years several predictive communication aids, based on the ideas developed in the research already described, have become commercially available. Most integrate character and word prediction into general-purpose writing aids. Some can in addition generate spoken output and control external devices such as telephones, televisions, and lights. Several systems are reviewed here. All of them are software products for the IBM PC, and most allow users to operate standard software through the predictive interface. In addition to these systems, commercial versions of the PAL and CDC systems described in Section 2.3 are available; the commercial version of CDC is called PACA, Portable Anticipatory Communication Aid. PAL is available from Scetlander Ltd., and PACA is available from Zygo Industries, Inc. (see Appendix D).

Cintex (available from NanoPac, Inc. [see Appendix D]) is an integrated environmental control system that incorporates an updated version of the CDC system in which the canonical word memory is replaced by an adaptive list, initially primed with the old canonical list but capable of forgetting unused words and replacing them with the user's own. It supports a variety of input devices – from one to four switches, joystick, keyboard, voice recognition – and provides both letter and word prediction. Letter predictions are based on fixed n-gram tables, and five predicted next letters are presented at a time. Word completions are also available. Once a letter is selected, the system displays the most common words beginning with that letter, as well as the newly predicted letters. The set of words offered is refined as the prefix grows. The system is advertised as having "artificial intelligence," apparently because it automatically adapts to the user's vocabulary by adding new words to its dictionary; these are offered in recency order. This improves upon the original CDC system, which had separate "core" and "learning" dictionaries and offered core words first.

Handikey is a switch-operated scanning matrix that can accommodate a variety of different input devices. The user is offered the option of single-switch or "automatic" scanning, dual-switch or "manual" scanning, and direct selection using a device such as a trackball, mouse, joystick, or head-mounted pointer. Handiword is a similar device, used with an external keyboard (or equivalent input device). Handikey and Handiword are both available from Microsystems Software, Inc. (see Appendix D). Both incorporate a built-in prediction facility that automatically determines those words in a dictionary that are most frequently used and makes them readily available. With Handikey, six predicted word completions are added to a special line of the display matrix. Handiword creates a one-line menu of up to nine words that are selectable using the numeric keypad. The user controls whether the menu is constantly displayed (called "persistent mode") or not (called "on-demand mode"). Both systems are dictionary-based, and are supplied with a standard vocabulary that the user can augment by pressing a special key once the word to be added has been entered in the normal way. New words can be added to one of several application-specific dictionaries, without leaving the current MS-DOS application program.

Help-U-Key, Help-U-Type, Help-U-Keyboard, and Freedom-Writer are members of the Helpware family of applications from World Communications (see Appendix D). The first two are similar to Handikey and Handiword. Help-U-Keyboard is a keyboard emulator; it displays a keyboard on the screen with which one can "type" by making selections with a mouse or similar device. Freedom-Writer is a stand-alone word processor that can use either direct selection or scanning inputs. All four systems offer 10 word completions at a time. Predictions are based on a 2,500-word dictionary, which does not adapt but is explicitly modifiable using a special key to add newly entered words. All but Freedom-Writer also offer (at extra cost) the option of "intelligent" next-word prediction, which can present up to 5 words most likely to follow the current one. The word-pairing is done from the user's input whenever two consecutive dictionary selections are made – this means that both words must be present in the dictionary. Surprisingly, Help-U-Key and Freedom-Writer, as well as Handikey, present the letters in their scanning matrix in alphabetic rather than frequency order, thus missing a fundamental level of predictive capability.

The Words+ family (available from Words+ Inc. [see Appendix D]) of communication aids resembles Helpware. It includes an oversized keyboard, a standard keyboard, a Morse code keyboard emulator, a scanning keyboard emulator, a direct selection keyboard emulator using a head pointer, and a stand-alone communication aid. Most of these systems provide two levels of prediction: word completion and next-word prediction (called "adaptive" word prediction). Word completion is based on a canonical, but user-modifiable, dictionary of between 3,000 and 5,000 words; up to six completions are presented on a pop-up menu. The "adaptive" word prediction presents the 6 words most likely to follow the just-selected one, based on the more recent word pairs that have been used so far. Of course, both words must already be in the dictionary.

Mindreader (available from Brown Bag Software [see Appendix D]) is a stand-alone word processor that is also advertised as using "artificial intelligence" to learn and make predictions. It employs automatic modeling to augment its predictions as you type – "the more you use it the smarter it gets." It offers a menu of four predictions, containing words and, sometimes, phrases. The exact mechanism used for predicting is not specified.

Various general-purpose operating system command interfaces incorporate command completion techniques. Possibly the first widely used one was the TENEX operating system described by Bobrow et al. (1972), which completed commands from an initial prefix whenever the user hit the escape key. One general-purpose interface that uses *adaptive* word completion is the GNU EMACS text editor found in Stallman (1981), which has a command called "dabbrevexpand" that offers completions for the current word by cycling through previously typed words with the same prefix, in recency order. Both these systems require the user to request completion explicitly rather than showing alternative predictions by default.

2.5. Summary and further reading

This chapter introduced the concept of predictive text generation and illustrated how predictive systems differ from their nonpredictive counterparts by incorporating prediction rules and dynamically conditioned prompting displays. They were shown to have several desirable characteristics and relatively few disadvantages. Existing systems were surveyed in three categories: letter anticipators, word or phrase completors, and combined systems. The burgeoning array of personal computer communication aids that incorporate prediction has been demonstrated by describing a handful of such systems.

The two main problems facing the designers of adaptive n-gram based predictive systems are how to create a memory that has experienced truly "representative" text to ensure accurate predictions, and how to display predictions to the user for rapid selection. These are the problems of model *construction* and model *consultation* respectively and are discussed in more detail in Part II.

The three-way categorization of predictive communication aids into letter anticipators, word completors, and combined systems was introduced by Darragh (1988). Of the letter anticipators covered here, the TIC and ANTIC systems were developed at Tufts New England Medical Center and are described by Baletsa et al. (1976), Baletsa (1977), Thomas (1980, 1981), and Demasco and Foulds (1982). MCCS, from Northwestern University, is presented by Heckathorne et al. (1980), Gibler (1981), and Gibler and Childress (1982). It seems that the Tufts and Northwestern groups collaborated and shared research results. DM was invented independently by Jones (1981).

The MAC word completor is described by Clarkson and Poon (1982), and the MOD system by Nelson et al. (1983, 1984). Recent accounts of PAL can be found in Newell (1989) and Newell et al. (1991). ISP/1 was developed by Colby and co-workers (Colby, 1984; Colby et al., 1978, 1982). The combined CDC system is described by Heckathorne and Childress (1982, 1983), and the portable PACA system that is based on it by Heckathorne et al. (1987). The speech-to-text/text-to-speech telephone communication system mentioned at the end of Section 2.1 is described by Stevens et al. (1984).

The famous "know the user" dictum is due to Hansen (1971), and the notion of "visual discontinuity" can be attributed to Foley and Wallace (1974). The idea of "dialogue determination" was espoused by Thimbleby (1980). Norman (1983) provides a useful compilation of general rules concerning user interface design, while Thimbleby (1990) contains a comprehensive discussion of most aspects of user interface design. Soede and Foulds (1986) discuss the trade-off between motor activity and mental load that is inherent in communication aids using prediction.

Language redundancy in general, and n-grams in particular, are discussed by Shannon (1951), Cover and King (1978), Suen (1979), and, in the context of communication aids, by Foulds et al. (1975) and Gibler (1981). The predictive model for the ANTIC system was derived from an unpublished analysis by Dr. E. Newman of Harvard University of a quarter of a million characters of written American English. According to Baletsa et al. (1976), these data were composed equally of the Holy Bible, writings of E. B. White, and *Saturday Review*. A less idiosyncratic corpus of American English text has been analyzed and made available by Kucera and Francis (1967). Cress (1986) provides a bibliography of studies of word usage frequency and vocabulary analysis.

Several groups are investigating the use of syntactic and semantic information to augment predictive capability, although only small improvements in predictive accuracy have been achieved. For example, syntax was used to enhance the PAL system (Arnott et al., 1984; Swiffin et al., 1987a, 1987b). A group in Sweden that has been working on predictive communication systems since 1983 is exploring the use of semantic and syntactic information (Hunnicutt, 1990; see also Magnuson and Hunnicutt, 1990; Rosengren and Hunnicutt, 1990). The "intelligent" and "adaptive" next-word prediction of Helpware and Words+ appears to be derived from the earlier work of Hunnicutt (1986, 1987). Yang et al. (1990) are investigating the use of semantic "tree adjoining grammars" to improve predictive ability.

Lazzaro (1990) surveys the use of personal computers for disabled people. Consumer demand for predictive facilities has made their provision by communication aid manufacturers a marketing necessity, although the bandwagon effect has inevitably led to loose use of the word *prediction*.

Other predictive systems for text entry include Freeboard, from Pointer Systems, Inc. (see Appendix D), and Predictive Typing, from Clwyd Technics Ltd. (see Appendix D).

3

The Predict system and its evaluation

About the same time that the earlier predictive text generation systems discussed in Chapter 2 were being developed, an unrelated line of research led to the creation of two novel systems at the University of Calgary. Predict was implemented in 1982 and is described in this chapter, along with some human factors experiments that were conducted to evaluate its effectiveness. This work led directly to the more sophisticated Reactive Keyboard concept presented in the remaining chapters of the book.

3.1. The Predict system

Predict is an experimental predictive text generation system that is designed as an operating system interface. Its key features are listed in Table 3.1. Predict uses a conventional QWERTY keyboard and visual display unit for input and output. It is implemented on a Digital Equipment Corporation VAX 11/780 minicomputer running the UNIX time-sharing operating system.

Adaptive fixed-length models, derived automatically from user inputs, are used to predict characters about to be typed. A string of predicted characters is displayed in reverse video following the current cursor position, and the user has the option of accepting correct predictions using special *accept-character, accept-word,* and *accept-line* function keys. The display then appears as though users had typed the predictions themselves. Incorrect predictions are eradicated by simply typing over them, in which case a new prediction might be displayed in its place. Table 3.2 describes the use of the system, and is in fact adapted from Predict's online help message.

A similar user interface was later adopted for the "Efficient Keyboard," a canonically defined word completor for deaf people. One or more initial letters of a typed word might cause one of 250 progressively refined word completions to appear automatically at the current cursor position. Correct predictions were either accepted with the space bar – which also added a space after the word – or implicitly rejected by typing over them.

Length-k modeling

Predict has its roots in a technique called "length-k modeling," which stores information about fixed-length sequences or "k-tuples," each k elements long, as they occur in an input sequence. Individual elements might be letters, words, or any other lexical items. Length-k models are essentially the same as n-gram models (with $n = k$), and are used in the same way. The current $k - 1$ elements form a

Table 3.1. *Key features of the Predict system*

System type	Keyboard emulator writing aid
Output device	VAX-11/780 (host)
Selection algorithm	Combined predictive text generation
Length (strokes/selection)	Decreases through acceleration
Cost (selections/word)	Decreases through amplification
Model type	Combination
Model construction	Automatic and explicit
Model consultation	Partially automatic
Model order (k)	3 to 10 or more
Model size	All addressable memory (typically 1 Mbyte)
Model source	User inputs and priming files
Source size	No limit
Confidence parameter	Not used

Table 3.2. *Online help provided for Predict*

Keys

F1	Accept complete prediction
F2	Accept one element of prediction
F3	Clear prediction memory
F4	Character mode (*default*)
F5	String mode
F6	Word mode
F7	Suspend predictor
F8	Exit
F9	Print this list

Warning

^D is not read

Predict does not work with screen-oriented programs (*emacs, fred, more, man* . . .)

Environment changes may produce side effects

Hint

If terminal modes become reset, execute `stty cbreak -nl -echo`

Execute `set term=tty` to minimize disruption to screen-oriented programs

Status

Model order = 4; confidence = 1

Character mode

context that is used to retrieve likely continuations from long-term memory. Whenever a prediction is required, those k-tuples are retrieved whose first $k - 1$ elements match the last-seen $k - 1$ elements of the sequence, and the k'th elements of these tuples are the various predictions.

The difference between length-k and n-gram models is really one of connotation only. First, the original investigations of length-k modeling in the 1970s emphasized the economical storage of models by using finite-automaton representations; this is largely irrelevant today with the vastly increased storage capacity that is readily available. Second, while n-gram models are usually built on individual *characters,* length-k ones are neutral with respect to the individual elements being modeled.

Predict stores three separate length-k models and can operate in three modes – single-character, word, and string. *Words* are defined as concatenations of alphanumeric characters separated by any other symbol, whereas *strings* are separated by white space and have no restriction on their constituent characters. Predict attempts to make predictions after each input character in character mode, after each word delimiter (i.e., nonalphanumeric character) in word mode, and after each string delimiter (i.e., space, tab, or end-of-line character) in string mode. It does not attempt to make predictions if the current context has not been encountered before, or if the end-of-line character is imminent. As we will see, character mode turns out to be the most successful.

Concatenated character predictions

Multiple acceptance keys and concatenated predictions extend character-mode Predict from a simple n-gram based letter anticipator to a combined predictive text generation system. Single letters, subword fragments, word completions, and even an entire line of characters can be accepted whenever a prediction is displayed. Each prediction is in fact a concatenated series of separately predicted character elements and can be accepted in whole or in part.

Progressively longer concatenations are formed as follows. First, using the current context, a character prediction is made and added to the display buffer. Then, it is assumed that this prediction is correct and destined to be accepted, and further predictions are made by "shifting" a copy of the context to form the new future context and repeating the process from the beginning. This continues until a novel context, or the end-of-line character, or the last screen column position, is encountered. The maximum length of a prediction therefore varies depending on the current cursor column position – up to 75 characters may be predicted at a time.

For example, if the current context HAP predicted the letter P, then P would be assumed correct and the context shifted to APP. APP would then be used to predict another letter, say Y, and the process repeated with the new projected context PPY. If no further elements were predicted, the concatenation PY would be displayed in reverse video at the cursor, following the HAP.

Frequency vs. recency

In cases where a given context of $k - 1$ elements retrieves several alternative k'th element predictions, a decision heuristic must be applied to determine which option to display. The choice affects the course of future contexts and predictions. There are two criteria on which the decision might be based: *frequency* and *recency*. The first would select the prediction that has occurred most often in the past, whereas the second would select that alternative that followed the current context on its last occurrence.

Predict uses a simple recency-based prediction heuristic equivalent to storing only the most recent k'th element for each $k - 1$ context. It maintains a record of how often each prediction has been made correctly. This record was used to investigate the effect of more conservative prediction strategies (see the "confidence" parameter below).

Correcting errors

Predict updates its three models after each new element is generated, whether typed in or accepted, so that current entries can have an immediate effect upon predictions. Of course, an aid that learns its user's *mistakes* will not be very helpful. In order to minimize assimilation of errors, each model is duplicated at the end of every new line of text to serve as a backup for the next line. Typing errors made while entering a line of text can be corrected before the line is completed by using backspace and line-delete keys. Revised length-k models are automatically regenerated from the backup copies as each change is made. A simpler strategy would have been to delay model updates until each line is completed, in a similar manner to MOD's word holding buffer.

Predict in use

As an example of the use of Predict, Figure 3.1 illustrates its operation on a command interaction with the UNIX operating system, starting in a completely unprimed state with k set to 4. The left column shows the commands that the user wishes to enter. This is a typical dialog – or rather, monolog, because the system's output is not shown – with UNIX, but it is not necessary to understand the meaning of the individual commands. On the right is a representation of the predictions that the system makes, with the symbol ⌐ standing for a correctly predicted character and ▌ standing for a point where the predictions become incorrect.

For example, the first prediction, the space on the third line, is correct but is immediately followed by incorrect predictions – in fact, a repetition of the first line was predicted. On the sixth line the `-1` after `ls` is predicted; on the next two lines the filename `test2` is completed automatically; but on the line after that `test2` is predicted where `test*` is desired. As can be seen, toward the end of the interaction a large proportion of characters are predicted correctly, with a sprin-

```
cd ..                              cd ..
ls                                 ls
cd modeling                        cd□modeling
ls -l                              ls -l
rm *.o y.tab.c                     rm *.o y.tab.c
ls -l test2                        ls□□□ test2
cat test2                          cat te□□□
pr test2|opr                       pr te□□□|opr
echo test*                         echo te□□▮*
rm test*                           rm▮te□□□
ls -l                              ls□□□▮
rm tty tty.out                     rm□□▮ty tt□▮.out
man compact                        man compact
newgrp bin                         newgrp bin
cd ..                              cd□▮..
man compact                        m a□□□□□□□□□
du                                 du
cd ../bin                          cd□□□/bin
cd bin                             cd□▮bi□
ls                                 ls▮
cat bib.make                       ca□□▮bi▮b.make
cd ../modelinα                     cd□▮.□□▮mod□□□□□
→ cp ../bib.make test3             cp ..□▮b□▮b□□□□□ te□□▮3
cp ../bin/bib.make test3           cp□□□□□□▮n/bi▮b□□□□□□□□□□
compact test3                      com□□□□ t□□□□
ls -l                              ls□□□
od -c test3.c                      od -c te□□□.c
od -c test3.C                      o d□□□□□□□□□□□▮C
pr test3.C ../bin/bib.make|opr     pr□□□□□□□□ ..□□□▮n□□□▮b□□□□□▮|op□
pr ../bin/bib.make|opr             pr□▮..□□□▮n□□□▮b□□□□□□□□
od -c test3.C|pr|opr               od□□□□□□□□□□□▮|pr|op□
rm test3.C                         rm□▮te□□□□□▮
ls -l ../bin                       ls□□□ ▮..□□□▮n▮
cat ../bin/bib.indiv               ca□□▮..□□□□/□□▮b▮.▮indiv
cp ../bin/bib.indiv test4          cp□□□□□□▮n□□□▮b□□□□□□ te□□▮4
pr test4|opr                       pr□▮t□□□□|op□
compact test4                      c o□□□□□□□□□□□▮
od -c test4.C                      o d□□□□□□□□□. C
od -c test4.C|pr|opr               o d□□□□□□□□□□□|□□□□□□
cd ../predictor                    cd□□□□▮predictor
```

Figure 3.1. Predict in operation (□ and ▮ indicate correct and incorrect predictions respectively).

kling of incorrect ones. In this example, many of the incorrect predictions arise from the coincidental lexical similarity of /bin and /bib. Most of this confusion would have been eliminated had k been set to 5.

There is an interesting occurrence in the line halfway down, marked with an arrow. Those with some knowledge of UNIX dialogs will readily infer that the user made an error in typing the second b in cp ../bib.make test3 – the line that follows, namely cp ../bin/bib.make test3, should have been typed instead. In fact, the system predicts that the line will begin cp ../bin rather than cp ../bib, and this discrepancy is marked as an error in the right-hand column.

But it is the dialog, not the prediction, that is in error. If the user had accepted the prediction, the mistake would not have been made because the system was prompting with the correct character. As this example illustrates, an adaptive predictive text generation system is capable of forestalling errors by presenting the user with correct predictions.

It is worth emphasizing that before this dialog began, Predict had no knowledge whatsoever of the form or content of the interaction it was about to model. Although illustrated with a command-line dialog, it works with any kind of text. However, command lines make a particularly good illustration because it is easy to see the system catching on to particular commands, filenames, and so on.

3.2. Assessing predictive power

Early simulation studies of Predict used a variety of model lengths, operating modes, levels of confidence, and genres of source text to probe the system's behavior. Several tests were undertaken to study how the relative success of prediction is affected by varying these parameters. All test runs were done with Predict's long-term memory initially empty – in other words, unprimed.

Mode and length

Predict was tested using character, word, and string mode, and with different values of k, on the same terminal session as was discussed previously (the left column of Figure 3.1). At any given character position, three events can occur: A prediction may not be attempted, it may be successful, or it may be incorrect. These three situations are depicted in Figures 3.2, 3.3, and 3.4 respectively.

The percentage of positions in which predictions are not attempted grows with the order of the model, because high-order models are less complete than low-order ones. Figure 3.2 plots this dependency for character, word, and string modes. In character mode, more predictions are attempted simply because there are more opportunities for prediction. Conversely, words and particularly strings, being longer tokens on average, present fewer opportunities to predict.

The percentage of positions in which correct predictions are made also decreases with model order, as can be seen in Figure 3.3. For any given order, character mode outperforms word mode, which itself outperforms string mode. The remaining positions, where predictions are made but are incorrect, are shown in Figure 3.4. Very few incorrect predictions are made by any of the models at orders greater than four.

The overall conclusion is that character models consistently outperform word-based or string-based models at each k-tuple length in the sense that, given any value for k in word or string mode, there is a value of k for which character mode yields more good predictions and fewer bad ones.

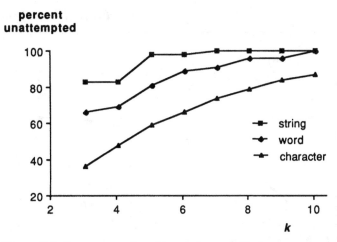

Figure 3.2. Percentage of positions where predictions were not attempted.

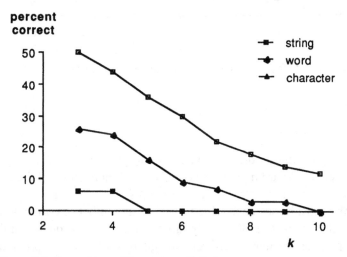

Figure 3.3. Percentage of correct predictions.

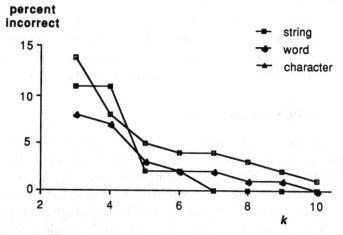

Figure 3.4. Percentage of incorrect predictions.

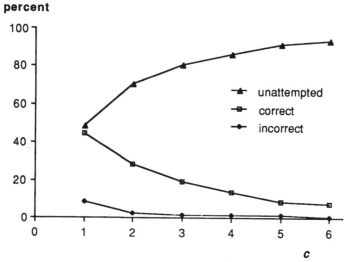

Figure 3.5. Effect of varying the confidence parameter *c*.

The "confidence" parameter

The effectiveness of any predictive text generation system – particularly one designed to augment keyboard input – rests on the user's perception of the usefulness of its predictions. It is clear from Figures 3.3 and 3.4 that when choosing a value for k, a compromise must be struck in which a sufficient number of correct predictions is generated without creating an unduly large number of bad ones. Predict has a "confidence" parameter c that specifies the length of run of correct predictions that must occur before a candidate prediction is displayed. If a predicted element is correct at least c consecutive times, it is considered safe to predict.

Figure 3.5 illustrates the effect of increasing c, with $k = 4$ in character mode, on the same test sequence. Incorrect predictions can be eliminated completely, but the price paid is a much smaller number of correct predictions. Because a large number of correct predictions was desired – even if more incorrect ones were generated – the confidence parameter was effectively abandoned by setting it to one.

Performance with different kinds of text

Predict was run on several different genres of input text to assess the influence of different vocabulary and syntax on prediction. Figure 3.6 illustrates the effect of increasing k, from three to eight, on the number of correct predictions made for each of three genres of text. Results are reported for the same terminal session test sequence as was used previously, a short program in the C programming language, and a scientific paper written in English. All values are for single-character mode

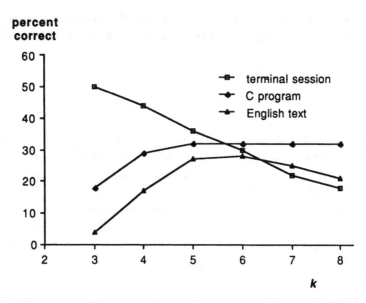

Figure 3.6. Correct predictions for three genres of text, plotted against *k*.

with $c = 1$. Increasing k up to six resulted in more correct predictions for C and for English – beyond six, performance leveled off or degenerated. Terminal session performance differed from C and English in that the success of predictions varied inversely with k for all values. This difference may be an artifact resulting from the relative brevity of the terminal session sample. Though marred by the lack of sample length control, these results – particularly for low values of k – probably reflect the differing degrees of statistical redundancy inherent in the three genres.

The main lessons learned from these early simulation studies are as follows. First, character mode consistently outperforms word and string modes. Second, the confidence parameter c is inappropriate for Predict's recency-based prediction strategy. Third, high-order models generally outperform low-order models on long test segments, whereas the reverse is true for short segments. Finally, the genre of input text has a great effect on Predict's ability to make correct predictions.

3.3. User pilot experiment

An exploratory study of Predict was undertaken to determine whether it had any measurable effect on users' performance of specific, well-controlled typing tasks, to collect users' impressions of the system, and to suggest ideas for ways to improve it. The task was to copy-type text using an ordinary line editor, to check it using a text comparison program, and to edit it until it was correct, rechecking after each line was corrected. A short fragment of English text and a short program written in the COBOL programming language were chosen as test samples; each one occupied less than a page. COBOL was chosen because it is notorious for its high degree of inherent redundancy.

Experimental design

The experiment was conducted on a VAX 11/750 running the UNIX operating system. All trials were started with Predict unprimed in character mode with $k = 4$. The recency-based decision heuristic was used, with $c = 1$ – in other words, no "confidence" parameter. Predict was started in a state identical to that which was used for the example depicted in Figure 3.1, the only difference being the text that was entered once it was running. The model was updated immediately as each character was typed, and regenerated from a backup if a line of text was edited during entry. All three acceptance modes (single letters, word completions, entire prediction) were available to the user. Operating the system seemed very straightforward to subjects; indeed, the clearly marked *help* key, which displayed the information in Table 3.2, was not used by any of the subjects during the course of the experiment.

Test sessions consisted of twice copy-typing a segment of text using the line editor, once with and once without prediction display. After subjects had copied each test sample they were instructed to use the line editing facility to correct any errors. Errors were located by repeatedly invoking a file comparison program that identified the first line of the copy that differed from the source document. A trial was finished when the copy was free from errors.

The control trial without predictions being displayed nevertheless had Predict running in the background, making invisible predictions and compiling user performance data. This also served to eliminate response time differences between trial types. The raw data collected from each trial consisted of copies of the completed line buffer contents, a record of keystroke and prediction activity, instantaneous keystroke rates, and line-by-line completion times.

A group of 23 paid able-bodied volunteers, fairly alike in terms of computer skill and experience, completed one practice and two test sessions each during the course of the experiment. Practice sessions allowed subjects to familiarize themselves with Predict, the line editor and text comparison programs, the general experimental procedure, and the two text genres used in the test sessions. During the test sessions subjects either worked with English in their first session and COBOL in their second or vice versa; prediction was either turned on for the first part of each session and off for the second or vice versa. To accomplish this, subjects were randomly assigned to one of the four counterbalanced streams shown in Table 3.3. Each session took between 15 and 30 minutes to complete.

Table 3.3. *Design of the pilot experiment*

Session		Stream		
	1	2	3	4
1	COBOL enabled/disabled	COBOL disabled/enabled	English enabled/disabled	English disabled/enabled
2	English enabled/disabled	English enabled/disabled	COBOL enabled/disabled	COBOL disabled/enabled

Hypotheses and results

Three dependent variables were initially derived from these data: the *keystroke per character ratio,* or number of keystrokes needed to complete a trial divided by the number of characters generated; the *character generation rate,* or number of characters generated divided by the time taken to complete the task; and the *number of errors,* measured by how often the comparison program was invoked (minus one for the final error-free comparison). These variables were used to test hypotheses based on the independent variables of *text type* (English or COBOL) and *prediction display* (predictions enabled versus predictions disabled). The null hypotheses were:

$H_{English}$ Users performing the typing task on identical English text will perform no differently with or without the prediction display.

H_{COBOL} Users performing the typing task on identical COBOL source code will perform no differently with or without the prediction display.

The real question is whether the predictions make any difference to user performance. To ensure a consistent system response time, predictions were made in all cases. The only difference between conditions for the predictions enabled and disabled was whether or not the predictions were shown to the user.

Table 3.4 summarizes the results of statistical tests (two-sided Student's t-tests) on the difference between these two prediction display states for each dependent variable. The only significant difference was found for the number of keystrokes needed per character when typing COBOL – predictions definitely reduced the number of keystrokes required for this task. (The figure of 1% in the table means that the likelihood that this result occurred by chance is less than 1 in 100.) On average, in the COBOL task, 86 keystrokes were needed to generate every 100 characters with predictions enabled, whereas with predictions disabled 108 keystrokes were required. With COBOL, having predictions displayed or not made no

Table 3.4. *Significance of predictions enabled vs.*
disabled: all subjects

	Predictions enabled vs. disabled	
Variable	English	COBOL
Keystrokes/character	n.s.	1%
Character generation rate	n.s.	n.s.
Number of errors	n.s.	n.s.

Note: n.s. means not significant

significant difference to the rate of character generation, or to the number of errors in the text. For English, no differences were found for any of the three measures. The result was that Predict had no measurable effect on the English task, but significantly reduced the keystroke/character ratio for the COBOL task.

The results from the pool of subjects were divided into three groups based on good, moderate, and poor typing ability. Typing skill level was determined from monitored character generation rates for the English task with prediction display disabled. Good, moderate, and poor groups had means of 3, 2, and 1.3 characters/second respectively. Each group was evaluated separately to determine which was most affected by Predict. The poorer typists benefited greatly when entering COBOL (the significance level, or probability that the effect occurred by chance, was less than 0.1%), whereas the moderate and good typists appeared to benefit less (significance level of 5% for both). Furthermore, although there was no overall reduction in character generation rate, the good typists may have been slowed down slightly (5% significance level).

Exploratory studies

A large number of exploratory studies were conducted to discover general trends in the data. A total of approximately 200 post hoc correlations and other statistical tests were made to compare differences between several dependent variables in various *prediction display, text type,* and *task phase* conditions. Note, however, that in such a large battery of tests, some statistically significant results are likely to occur purely by chance.

First, the recorded data were divided into the *entry* stage, where the user is copy-typing text in the first place, and the *edit* stage, where it is edited until it passes the file-comparison test. The significant reduction that predictions produced in the COBOL keystroke/character ratio (86 vs. 108 keystrokes) occurred exclusively in the entry phase of the task. Statistical tests showed no significant differences between predictions enabled and disabled for either phase of the English task, or for the edit phase of the COBOL task.

One counterintuitive result was that displaying predictions and allowing the user to respond to them seemed to interfere with Predict's ability to make correct predictions. For example, for COBOL the number of predictions generated per keystroke was 12% lower when predictions were enabled, and of these, fewer were correct (down by 10%). These reductions were statistically significant. Predict was correct 70% of the time when predictions were enabled and 80% of the time when they were not. No explanation was found for this surprising effect.

The typing rate measures of characters/time and keystrokes/time were strongly correlated between English and COBOL in the entry phase but not in the edit phase. Some fairly strong correlations were discovered between the way that users accepted predictions and the different task phases. *Accept-character* occurred primarily in the entry phase, *accept-word* in the edit phase. This may be because a more adequate model had been constructed by the time the edit phase is entered.

With predictions enabled, statistical tests indicated that more correct predictions per keystroke were made for COBOL (70%) than for English (42%). Of course, correct predictions are not necessarily accepted by the user: In fact, 42% of correct predictions were accepted for COBOL whereas only 15% were accepted for English. The poor quality of Predict's suggestions for English compared to COBOL may well have contributed to the fact that a lower proportion of correct predictions were accepted in this case.

For both COBOL and English the number of times the *accept-character* key was pressed was fairly strongly correlated with the number of correct predictions. The results showed significantly fewer correct predictions – and consequently more bad ones – during the English entry phase compared with the edit phase. The converse was true for COBOL.

The results of this analysis can be summarized as follows. First, for the COBOL task Predict performed better during the entry phase than in the edit phase. Second, a statistically significant reduction in keystroke/character ratio occurred only during the entry phase of the COBOL task. Third, COBOL led to more predictions, of which more were correct and more were accepted, relative to English. Finally, and surprisingly, simply displaying COBOL predictions reduced the proportion of correct predictions compared with those that were generated when prediction was disabled.

Feedback from subjects

After each test session, subjects were asked to complete a questionnaire comprising a series of limited-choice questions about their impressions and perceptions of Predict. Of the 23 subjects, approximately 60% liked the system and 20% were neutral; 50% said they found it helpful and 25% felt it had no effect. Over two-thirds wanted it to be publicly available so that they could use it in their regular work.

Table 3.5. *Summary of user suggestions and comments*

Suggestions for improving Predict
Make "better predictions"[a]
Faster system response (speed is critical)[a]
Display more than one choice at a time[a]
Include carriage return in predictions[a]
Exploit the frequency distribution of elements[a]
Improve tactile continuity (e.g., accept-key placement)[a]

Remove *accept-line* key (wasn't used)
Freedom to select what should be predicted
Have specialized systems for different languages
Don't predict leading or trailing white spaces
Have an audible tone announce prediction display

Additional comments
Nice for editing
Don't use for editing
Good for repeated sequences
Supply an explicit mental model to users
Very helpful with operating system commands
Composition rather than copying more appropriate
Helps to prevent spelling mistakes

No reason not to use it, easy to ignore
Seldom correct
Needs explicit modifiability to user preferences
Predictions were distracting
Test samples were too short
Only *accept-word* was useful

[a]Adopted for the Reactive Keyboard.

Most users stated that they had no difficulty adjusting to the system and adopted a strategy of either trying to anticipate "what it was going to predict" or ignoring predictions while copying. They generally found it good for working with the highly repetitive COBOL text sample where it had "very useful and predictable behavior." The main criticism, which came from approximately one-third of the subjects, was the visually demanding nature of the system and the concomitant visual discontinuity – a particular concern for those who were not touch typists. Some suggested that watching the screen slowed them down, though no significant speed differences were detected in the data.

Approximately half of the subjects responded to a request for recommendations on ways to improve the system; the other half thought it was fine as it was. Their suggestions are in Table 3.5. Those suggestions that were later incorporated into the Reactive Keyboard are noted. The consensus was for better predictions – more correct ones – and faster system response time, and various suggestions were offered for new ways to present and accept predictions.

Most subjects gave additional open-ended comments at the end of each questionnaire. Those differing from earlier suggestions are also listed in Table 3.5. Overall, comments were favorable. Most subjects "found it quite nice"; two "found it annoying." Interestingly, some subjects felt that Predict was most useful for editing, whereas others felt that it was ill-suited to editing. The COBOL task, with its inherent redundancy, was widely favored over English. Many stated that an explicit mental model of the Predict algorithm would have enhanced their ability to anticipate and acknowledge correct predictions – some thought, incorrectly, that it worked on the basis of word completion.

Finally, many subjects from each skill level thought that they could enter text quicker with the predictive interface than without it, even though predictions had no measurable effect on character entry rate for poor and moderate typists, and actually slowed down the better typists. This remarkable result makes one wonder whether the goal should be to improve productivity or to improve the perception of productivity!

Evaluating adaptive systems such as Predict is a challenging task. It is complicated by the large number of variables to be controlled and the nondeterministic nature of adaptive systems in general. Altering the system's parameters and experimental conditions can lead to vastly different or conflicting results. The experimental conditions were in fact strongly biased *against* Predict. The copy task in itself is ill-suited to the visually demanding nature of a predictive text generation system. The use of short text segments and the absence of long-term memory priming limited Predict's ability to form adequate models. This forced the use of a low value of k, namely $k = 4$, so that at least some predictions could be made during the course of the experiment. The recency-based decision heuristic further constrained Predict's potential power. Another complicating factor was the often sluggish system response time imposed by the time-shared environment. It is mildly surprising then that the results of the pilot experiment were so favorable, in terms of both objective results – the COBOL keystroke/character ratio – and user satisfaction.

3.4. The different faces of Predict

The Predict mechanism is quite general and can be applied in many situations. For example, when used at the UNIX command level (Figure 3.1) it becomes a form of automatic programming assistant. When used for English or COBOL it takes on the appearance of a device specially adapted to these environments.

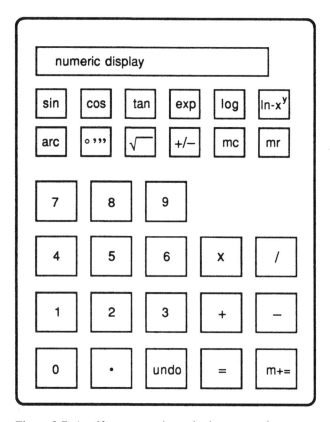

Figure 3.7. A self-programming calculator. mc, clear memory;
mr, retrieve from memory; m+=, add to memory.

One quite different application that has been investigated is as an interface to an electronic calculator. Consider the simple, nonprogrammable pocket calculator (Figure 3.7). By arranging for Predict to "look over your shoulder" while you use it for a repetitive task, it is possible after a while for it to predict the keys that will be pressed next. Any that cannot be predicted correspond to "input." Thus the system can eventually behave exactly as though it had been explicitly programmed for the task at hand, waiting for the user to enter a number, and simulating the appropriate sequence of key presses to come up with the answer.

The calculator constructs an adaptive model of the sequence of keys the user presses. If the task is repetitive (like computing a simple function for various argument values), Predict will soon catch on to the sequence and begin to activate the keys itself. Inevitably the prediction will sometimes be wrong, and an *undo* key allows the user to correct errors.

Figure 3.8 gives some examples of this "self-programming" calculator. The first sequence shows the evaluation of xe^{1-x} for a range of values of x. The keys pressed

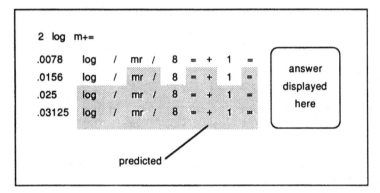

(a)

(b)

(c)

Figure 3.8. Examples of operation of the self-programming calculator: (a) evaluating xe^{1-x} for various values of x, (b) evaluating $1 + \log x / 8 \log 2$ for various values of x, and (c) evaluating a more complex expression.

by the operator are in normal type; those predicted by the system are shaded. From halfway through the second iteration onward, the device behaves as though it had been explicitly programmed for the job. It waits for the user to enter a number, and displays the answer. It takes slightly longer for the constant 1 to be predicted than the preceding operators because numbers in a sequence are more likely to change than operators. Therefore the system requires an additional confirmation before venturing to predict a number. In other words, the "confidence" parameter of Section 3.2 is set to two for digits and one for other keys. Figure 3.8b shows the evaluation of

$$1 + \frac{\log x}{8 \log 2}$$

for various values of x. The first line stores the constant log 2 in memory. More complicated is the evaluation of

$$20 + 10 \log \left[1 + a^2 - 2a \cos \frac{180x}{4000} \right] - 10 \log \left[1 + a^2 - 2a \cos 45 \right]$$

for $a = 0.9$. Because the calculator possesses only one memory location, it is expedient to compute the last subexpression first and jot down the result. The result of this calculation (−2.69858) only has to be keyed twice before the system picks it up as predictable. Some interference occurs between this initial task and the main repeated calculation, for three suggestions had to be "undone" by the user. The negative effect of one of these "undo's" continues right up until near the end of the interaction. This means that the penultimate "+" on each line has to be keyed by the user several times to counter the system's reluctance to predict it.

3.5. Summary and further reading

Predict was one of the first truly adaptive predictive systems that built its model automatically from user inputs – the Dynamic Matrix described in Chapter 2 was another early example. Predict's origin as a length-k modeler led to the innovative concept of concatenated character predictions that could be accepted in whole or in part. It nevertheless has several shortcomings in addition to its many conceptual advantages (Table 3.6). The second part of this book introduces the Reactive Keyboard, which was the direct result of efforts to capitalize on Predict's strengths and overcome its weaknesses.

The length-k modeling technique is discussed by Witten (1979, 1981a) and has its roots in Andreae's (1977, 1984) PUSS robot learning system. Predict was originally described by Witten (1982) and Witten et al. (1982). The "Efficient Keyboard," which has a similar user interface, is described by Stevens et al. (1984). The experimental study described in the text was undertaken by students

Table 3.6. *Advantages and shortcomings of Predict*

Advantages
Uses adaptive, automatic long-term memory formation
Concatenated predictions and multiple acceptance keys
Exploits subword fragments and interword redundancies
Character (or symbol) set independent
Prediction length limited only by screen width

Shortcomings
Uses fixed-length models (larger k means slower learning)
Uses recency-based decision rule (instead of frequency)
Only one (if any) prediction alternative displayed
Is often unable to make a prediction
Does not predict beyond the end-of-line character
Does not interact well with screen-oriented programs

and faculty involved in a human factors graduate course at the University of Calgary in 1982. The self-programming calculator is described by Witten (1981b). For information on the C programming language and the UNIX operating system, see Kernighan and Ritchie (1978) and Ritchie and Thompson (1974) respectively.

PART II

The Reactive Keyboard

4
The user interface

> *To originate is to combine.*
> — *Edgar Allan Poe*

The Reactive Keyboard is a device that accelerates typewritten communication with a computer system by predicting what the user is going to type next. Several different versions have been implemented. To simplify the design, a clear distinction has been made between the interface and the prediction mechanism; this chapter concentrates on the former. Different user interfaces are required for different computers, different types of application, and – most important – different residual communication abilities possessed by the user. In order to encourage the creation of new interfaces, Chapter 6 presents and documents the code that forms the core of the prediction mechanism used in all versions.

Unlike Predict, which attempted, at best, single predictions and was often unable to suggest a prediction, the Reactive Keyboard always makes available a menu of different predictions. Each prediction starts with a different character, and is a character string obtained by concatenating successive single-character predictions. Menu items are presented in frequency order so that the most likely ones appear first.

There are two basic styles of interface that differ according to how many menu items are displayed. There are also two basic styles of selecting from the menu: using function keys and using a proportional input device like a mouse. In conjunction with a proportional input device, the Reactive Keyboard is well-suited to many severely disabled users because text can be generated *solely* by selecting from a menu of predicted continuations, without resorting to a keyboard. These interface styles are discussed further in Section 4.2.

To improve the predictions themselves, the Reactive Keyboard's model is stored in a special tree structure that enables *variable length* matches to be made between short- and long-term memory. Recall from Chapter 2 that short-term memory records the current context, which is used to retrieve likely continuations from long-term memory. *Partial matching* allows better predictions to be made before a complete higher-order model is constructed, and helps to overcome the problem of incomplete statistical characterization of the text being entered. These mechanisms are discussed in Chapter 5.

Here we look at general interface issues and examine incarnations of the Reactive Keyboard for UNIX, MS-DOS, and the Apple Macintosh computer systems.

69

Table 4.1. *Differences between Predict and the Reactive Keyboard*

Feature	Predict	Reactive Keyboard
Long-term memory structure	Hash table	Variable-length tree
Short-term memory context	Fixed length, $k - 1$	Variable length, $k - 1$ to 0
Prompting device	VDU	VDU or dual-window display
Menu presentation	Single item available	128 menu items available
Input device	Keyboard	Keyboard or pointer
Buttons B	QWERTY + 3	Proportional or QWERTY + ~25
Selection elements N	Created adaptively	Created adaptively
k-tuple elements	Letter, word, string	ASCII characters
Frequency counts	2^{32} maximum	2^7 maximum
Selection elements	Concatenated elements	Concatenated characters
Error correction	Line edit and recency	Frequency and forgetting
Decision rule	Recency-based	Frequency based
Forgetting	Recency only	Frequency halving
Zero-frequency problem	Doesn't predict	Rank, then ASCII order
Global contexts	One only	Multiple possible

4.1. Predict and the Reactive Keyboard

Predict and the Reactive Keyboard have a number of features in common. Both are expressive communication aids devised to facilitate and accelerate overall fluency. They are both designed as keyboard-emulating writing aids with the aim of decreasing the average number of strokes per selection (i.e., "length" as defined in Chapter 1) and the average number of selections per word (i.e., "cost") of interactive text generation. Both use a selection method that employs automatic and explicit model construction, and partially automatic model consultation. In practice the order of the model lies between $k = 3$ and $k = 10$, although there is no theoretical limit to the value of k, or to the size of the model, or to the amount of representative text that is used to prime it. Beyond these general resemblances, there are some major differences inspired by the suggestions for improving Predict (Table 3.5). The key points involve issues affecting prediction generation and display.

Table 4.1 lists the differences between Predict and the Reactive Keyboard and illustrates how the suggestions in Table 3.5 are implemented. Foremost are:

use of a flexible tree-structured memory

variable-length, or "partial," context matching to improve prediction in the absence of complete higher-order models exploitation of a dual-window display, separating the prompting display from the host message area

a two-dimensional prompting device menu, allowing selection of both the item and the number of characters to be taken from it

suitable for use with a proportional input device

A number of changes were made to the way in which the consequences of automatic modeling are handled. The decision heuristic is now based on frequency rather than recency; forgetting is accomplished by halving popularity counts rather than by storing the most recent entry only; and the zero-frequency problem is handled using rank order followed by ASCII collating order, whereas Predict does not attempt predictions for novel contexts. Moreover, low popularity and eventual forgetting provide a degree of automatic error correction over and above Predict's line buffer editing.

Some of these advances, taken individually, have precedents in other systems. For example, both MOD and ISP/1 can use proportional input devices, and the Dynamic Matrix uses a similar tree-structured memory. However, the Reactive Keyboard goes beyond these systems not only in how these features are exploited, but also in how they are combined. The resulting synergy is apparently unprecedented and seems to represent a conceptual advance over earlier predictive text generation systems.

4.2. Different faces of the Reactive Keyboard

Two different styles of user interface have been investigated: one relying on a keyboard (or, more generally, a set of buttons), called RK-Button, and the other using a mouse (or, more generally, any kind of pointer device), called RK-Pointer.

The keyboard style was originally designed for remote access to a host computer via a 1200 bit/second telephone link. It uses a standard terminal keyboard and screen as input and output devices. Because of the link's relatively low speed, predictions are presented at the host cursor one at a time. However, the user is able to step through and select any one of 128 different predictions. Versions are now available that assist with the command-line dialogs of both the UNIX and MS-DOS operating systems. RK-Button's principal functions and commands are in Table 4.2.

The mouse-based style has a separate menu of predictions from which selections are made using a proportional input device. Here the user selects not only a menu item, but also a point within it. The substring up to that point is inserted into the text buffer. For example, if the prompting display included the menu item "next prediction," then pointing to the letter "d" would insert the characters "next pred." This provides a kind of two-dimensional selection capability: The user chooses the menu item vertically, and the extent horizontally. The two-dimensional menu structure is presented on the screen and updated continually as selections are made. RK-Pointer has all the functionality summarized in Table 4.2 but provides access

Table 4.2. *RK-Button's functionality and commands*

Command type	Action
Selection control	Accept forward char
	Accept forward word
	Accept to end of line
	Previous prediction
	Next prediction
Display control	Show newlines
	Truncate at newlines
Model control	Prime from file
	Zero-frequency file
Error control	Beginning of line
	End of line
	Backward character
	Forward character
	Delete character
	Backspace character
	Discard rest of line
	Previous line
	Next line
Panic control	Help
External model manipulation	Modify primary file
	Alter zero-frequency table

to it through a simple point-and-click interface. It has been implemented as a simple stand-alone text editor for Apple Macintosh computer systems.

RK-Button

An interaction with UNIX using RK-Button is shown in Figure 4.1a. The outcome of the dialog appears in Figure 4.1c. Predicted characters are written in reverse video on the screen, and represented in the figure with enclosing rectangles. Control characters are preceded by "^," and ^J is the end-of-line character. The column on the right shows the keys actually struck by the user. Figure 4.1b gives the meaning of a few of them; in fact, many more line-editing features are provided. Although not illustrated in the figure, the system is set up so that typing noncontrol characters simply overwrites the predictions. Thus one may use the keyboard in the ordinary way without even looking at the screen.

Figure 4.1a shows the entry of five command lines. Within each of the five groups preceded by the $ sign, each line actually overwrote its predecessor on the

(a)
```
$ mail^J                                              ^N
  cd news^J                                           ^W
  cd news^J                                           ^N
  cd rk/papers/ieee.computer^J                        ^L
  cd rk/papers/ieee.computer

$ emacs paper.tex^J                                   ^L
  emacs paper.tex

$ rm paper.tex.CKP paper.tex.BAK^J                    ^L
  rm paper.tex.CKP paper.tex.BAK

$ wc -w paper.tex^J                                   ^L
  wc -w paper.tex

$ readnews -n comp.sources.unix^J                     ^N
  mail^J                                              ^W
  mail^J                                              ^N
  mail bdarragh%uncamult.bitnet@ucnet.ucalgary.ca^J   ^L
  mail bdarragh%uncamult.bitnet@ucnet.ucalgary.ca
```

(b)
Key	Description
^C	Accept the next predicted character
^W	Accept the next predicted word
^L	Accept the whole predicted line
^N	Show the next alternative prediction
^P	Show the previous alternative prediction

(c)
```
$ cd rk/papers/ieee.computer
$ emacs paper.tex
$ rm paper.tex.CKP paper.tex.BAK
$ wc -w paper.tex
$ mail bdarragh%uncamult.bitnet@ucnet.ucalgary.ca
```

Figure 4.1. RK-Button in operation: (a) dialog with UNIX, (b) some commands, and (c) screen contents at the end of the dialog.

Figure 4.2. Maltron single-handed keyboard: (left hand) plug compatible for the IBM PC/AT (switchable) and keyboard-compatible machines. Courtesy of P.C.D. Maltron Ltd., Surrey, England.

screen. Consider the first group. After the first prediction, mail^J, the user struck ^N to show the next one. This prediction, cd#news^J, replaced the previous prediction on the screen. (We use the symbol "#" to make space visible.) The user accepted the first word of it, cd#, using the ^W command, moved to the next prediction, and accepted it in its entirety. The only thing remaining on the screen at this point was cd#rk/papers/ieee.computer. Following this, the next three commands were predicted in their entirety, whereas the last one required four keystrokes. The screen contents at the end of the dialog (less any output from the host computer) are shown in Figure 4.1c.

In summary, five command lines comprising a total of 138 characters were entered using 11 strokes on just three function keys – an average of 2.2 keystrokes per command line or 12.5 characters per keystroke. This is fairly typical for command-line dialogs with UNIX.

The original implementation of RK-Button was designed for the single-handed keyboard shown in Figure 4.2, a P.C.D. Maltron. The choice of control characters in Figure 4.1 originates from this system. However, control characters can be quite difficult to type, and different keyboards and key assignments will be preferred by

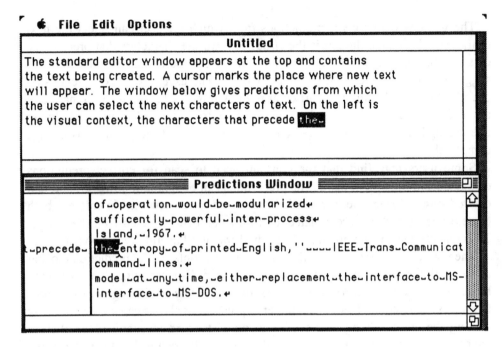

Figure 4.3. RK-Pointer in operation.

different people. On a conventional keyboard, the RK-Button functions are invariably bound to more convenient function keys. The program allows users to rebind them easily to different keys.

Predictions are based on the text provided to the Reactive Keyboard in the form of a priming file, as well as text entered in the current interactive session. For good performance it is essential for the priming file to match the type of text being entered. A default or user-specified priming file is read into the predictive model at start-up. In addition, the Reactive Keyboard can be reprimed at any time from a standard text file.

RK-Pointer

RK-Pointer embodies quite a different interface to the same prediction mechanism. Figure 4.3 shows a typical view of the screen when using a stand-alone text editor that incorporates it. When the Reactive Keyboard is invoked, two windows appear, as shown in the figure. Both of these windows can be scrolled, moved, and resized.

The "text window" (labeled "Untitled") appears at the top and contains the text being created. A cursor marks the place where new text will appear. Basic text editing facilities are provided for file handling and text manipulation. Only one text window can be open at a time.

The window below gives predictions from which the user can select the next characters of text. On the left is the *visual context,* the characters that precede the cursor in the text window. On the right is a menu of predictions that are offered as suggestions of how the context might continue. The user enters text by choosing one of these and clicking at a particular point within it. Characters up to that point are inserted into the upper window, and both context and predictions in the lower one are updated accordingly – the context moves on and the predictions change completely.

Some users may find that the constant need to scan for correct predictions distracts from the task at hand. The predictions can be ignored, however, and text entered directly from the keyboard. In any case, after new text is entered, both context and predictions are updated as if they had been selected with the mouse. Thus one can use the keyboard in the normal way until useful predictions appear.

The prediction window is scrollable, and always contains 128 predictions so that any ASCII character can be entered and users can dispense with a physical keyboard. Predictions are ordered by probability: The one beginning with the most likely next letter comes first. The number of predictions shown can be controlled by making the window longer or shorter using a standard mechanism for altering window size. The length of each prediction can be controlled by making the window wider or narrower. Of course, longer predictions are less likely to be grammatically correct, but they have greater potential for speeding text entry. The vertical line separating context and prediction can be grabbed and moved horizontally, so that the length of the context displayed in the prediction window can be varied as well. However, this is independent of the context length used for prediction, which is determined by the order of the model.

As the mouse is moved around over the prediction window, characters of the current prediction, up to the mouse position, are highlighted automatically so that one can always see exactly what would be entered if the mouse button were to be clicked ("the#" in Figure 4.3). Thus toying with the mouse causes the highlighting to change rapidly. Although this violates the normal Macintosh convention that changes only occur on mouse clicks, there seems to be ample justification for it in this interface.

The line of visual context in the prediction window moves up and down with the mouse so that it is always alongside the highlighted entry – the user sees the context leading into the current prediction. Also, that prediction is copied into the text window at the insertion point, providing additional selection feedback. However, this is only done when inserting at the end of the text buffer, to avoid the need to redraw continually the remaining part of the buffer. Characters preceding the cursor position can be erased by moving the mouse over the context string that is displayed to the left of the predictions.

Figure 4.4 illustrates the entry of several words of text in a sequence of eight screen images. For presentation purposes, the windows are rather small and are

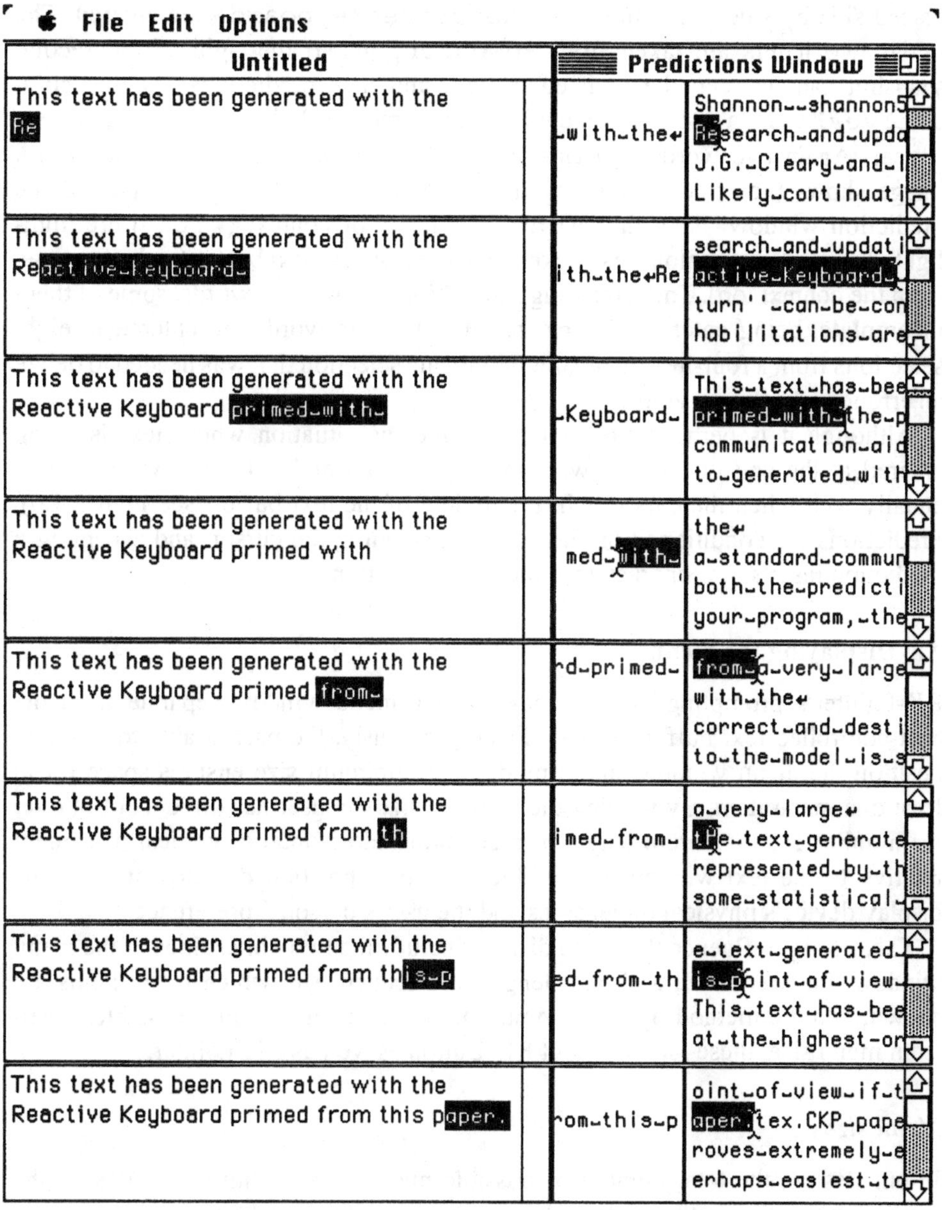

Untitled		Predictions Window
This text has been generated with the `Re`	`_with_the←` `Re`search	Shannon--shannonS `Re`search_and_upda J.G._Cleary_and_I Likely_continuati
This text has been generated with the Re`active_keyboard_`	`ith_the←Re` `active_Keyboard`	search_and_updati `active_Keyboard` turn''_can_be_con habilitations_are
This text has been generated with the Reactive Keyboard `primed_with_`	`_Keyboard_`	This_text_has_bee `primed_with_`the_p communication_aid to_generated_with
This text has been generated with the Reactive Keyboard primed with	`med_`with`_`	the← a_standard_commun both_the_predicti your_program,_the
This text has been generated with the Reactive Keyboard primed `from_`	`^d_primed_`	`from_`a_very_large with_the← correct_and_desti to_the_model_is_s
This text has been generated with the Reactive Keyboard primed from `th`	`imed_from_`	a_very_large← `th`e_text_generate represented_by_th some_statistical_
This text has been generated with the Reactive Keyboard primed from th`is_p`	`ed_from_th`	e_text_generated_ `is_p`oint_of_view_ This_text_has_bee at_the_highest-or
This text has been generated with the Reactive Keyboard primed from this p`aper.`	`^om_this_p`	oint_of_view_if_t `aper.`tex.CKP-pape roves_extremely_e erhaps_easiest_to

Figure 4.4. Several snapshots of the screen during text entry with RK-Pointer.

placed side by side. First, the words Reactive#Keyboard# are entered. The initial two letters are taken from Research, and to the right of the second snapshot can be seen the updated context and new predictions. At this point active#Keyboard# is entered with a single mouse click, and fresh predictions appear. Again two words – primed#with# – are entered together. The fourth image shows the effect of moving the cursor back into the context part of the prediction window: Now the last few characters of context (with#) are highlighted and, when the mouse is clicked, deleted from the text buffer (and, of course, from the context too). The remaining illustrations show more words, some of them incomplete, being entered. The net result is that six words are entered in eight selections from a four-item menu, including one selection that was needed to delete an erroneously chosen word.

Although it is perhaps easiest to envisage the situation where text is being entered at the end of the text window (Figures 4.3 and 4.4), the system works equally well when the cursor is in the middle of the text buffer (see Figure 4.6). Predictions are conditioned on the context preceding the cursor, and accepting a prediction inserts new characters at the cursor position.

4.3. Displaying the menu

RK-Pointer's prompting display consists of a menu window separate from the host-controlled text buffer. As mentioned previously, the user is able to size and position the menu window, and a predefined minimum size ensures space for at least one menu item. By varying the window size the user has direct control over the number and maximum length of predictions. Horizontal or vertical placement relative to the text window is possible. The best position depends on both the display device's physical dimensions and the user's personal preference.

Factors that influence the menu display include the two dimensions of the menu window, the menu size and item length, the sequence in which menu items are shown, and the method by which nonprinting characters are made visible. Apart from menu size, these factors affect RK-Button as well as RK-Pointer.

Menu size

In our design, the total number of possible menu items is limited to 128 by the restriction that the first letter of each item be unique. Obviously the minimum menu length is one item, whereas the maximum is governed by the number of lines displayable on the prompting device.

What is the best menu length? Human factors considerations would limit the number of items in a window to a maximum such as the "magic number" seven plus or minus two. This will necessitate splitting the menu display into several "pages." With representative priming, it is easy to achieve a very high number of first-page predictions with page lengths within this range. For example, menu-length simulation studies for various levels of priming have shown, by plotting the probability of first-page selection against menu length for a specific sample of text, that a window with ten items would contain virtually 100% of all desired initial characters if long-term memory was preprimed with the same text sample. Given excellent priming, even a menu as short as two items was shown to hold most of the desired characters on its first page. Even without any priming, on a fairly short 11,000 character passage, the first 10 items contained 69% of the desired initial letters. An important effect to be aware of is that decision time will increase with the number of choices available – Fitts' Law. In practice, menu size is left to each user's preference.

Item length

There are many different ways of determining the length of menu items. The minimum is one character, and the maximum is constrained by the width of the prompting device. Although it is desirable to minimize the average number of selections made by the user by presenting long items, there are other cognitive and psycholinguistic factors to be considered.

There are three different approaches to determining the item length:

use a fixed length that fills all available menu space

compute the length as a function of the prediction's popularity and/or the size of the context associated with retrieval of its initial character

base the length on perceptual units such as words or lines of text

The first method is the simplest, and offers the user the greatest potential selection productivity. A minimum length of approximately seven characters may be desirable based on the observation that a minimum preview size of seven letters is needed by normal subjects for efficient copy-typing.

The second is supported by evidence that the grammatical correctness of predictions increases with model order and decreases with prediction length. Moreover, it has some merit in that item length would provide feedback on the relative strength of competing predictions, although it does not add appreciable information when items are displayed in popularity order. Both these methods have the disadvantage of largely ignoring the grammatical structure of predictions and the significance of delimiting white space.

The third method takes these last factors into account by acknowledging the importance of perceptual units. For example, experience with RK-Button suggests that prediction beyond the new-line character is of little value in an environment in which commands are entered and executed line by line. The most general approach is to generate predictions of a predetermined maximum length and then truncate them to suit the particular psycholinguistic, display, and selection strategies in

Table 4.3. *Mean type and token lengths in a large sample of English text*

Value	Types		Tokens	
	Length (chars)	Types ≤ length	Length (chars)	Tokens ≤ length
Mean	8.13	—	4.74	—
Standard deviation	2.99	—	2.66	—
[mean]	8	45%	5	46%
[mean + 2]	10	70%	7	68%
[mean + 4]	12	86%	9	85%
[mean + 6]	14	94%	11	95%

Source: Derived from the Brown Corpus of Kucera and Francis (1967).

effect. One drawback is that item length may vary greatly due to the relative position of various delimiters.

Another approach to determining the most effective item length is to consider that the user will often be selecting word completions, and to base the length of menu items on the average length of words. The average word length in a text depends on whether one takes the average over the vocabulary used, that is the word "types," or over the full text itself, that is the word "tokens." Mean token length is equivalent to mean type length weighted by each word's frequency of occurrence. Table 4.3 shows mean type and token lengths plus two, four, and six characters, for a large sample of English text. Notice that the mean type length is nearly twice the mean token length, indicating that frequently used words are relatively short. These data suggest that a minimum length of about twelve characters is required to ensure that 85% to 90% of words could be presented unbroken in the menu.

About the same number of characters could be used as context feedback for word recognition in the menu buffer. Retaining a small number of characters aids item selection because the beginning letter or letters of a word, and its overall length, are primary visual cues to word discrimination, and are more important than word endings and internal letters or letter combinations. Also, word beginnings are less redundant than word endings and are valuable cues to word recognition.

Longer menu items may help decrease typographical errors by supplying correct predictions, thereby reducing overall error recovery time. Whether a user is distracted by overlong items is really a personal matter. Shorter menu items will break words more often. However, even if words are broken frequently, it is probably no more difficult to compose text out of word fragments than to spell it out letter by letter.

In practice, both the first technique (using a fixed length that fills the available menu space) and the last (basing the length on perceptual units such as lines of text) are implemented and the user can select between them. Current implementations of RK-Button are used to assist with command-line dialogs and it is natural to terminate predictions when the new-line character is encountered, because single lines are the basic unit of communication in this environment. In RK-Pointer, which is embedded in a text editor, the line may not be a natural unit of communication. The user is given explicit control over the maximum item length by resizing the window in which the menu is displayed.

Sequence of items

Once the number and length of menu items are determined, they must be placed in a sensible order on the prompting device. Clearly each succeeding menu page should contain items of decreasing likelihood, and current implementations simply present predictions in probability order.

There is considerable latitude for more elaborate ordering schemes within individual menu pages. One possibility is to order freshly generated menu pages in a way that minimizes disturbance of the old menu that is being replaced. Any initial characters that are common to the old menu would retain their original positions, while the remainder would be distributed in the remaining spots. This is a partial solution to the "moving target" effect, where users see where they want to make their *next* selection as well as the current one, but by the time they have an opportunity to make their next selection the display has been updated and the item has moved. It is also possible that cursor-centered placement, where items of highest probability are sited near the pointer's cursor, would speed selection. However, this depends on the kind of input device, cursor feedback mechanism, and the user's visual preference.

Displaying nonprinting characters

The final display issue to be considered is the representation of nonprinting characters. The solution adopted for RK-Button is the common convention of displaying control characters as a character pair, prefixing the uppercase rendition of the character with a "^." For example, the ASCII BEL (rings the terminal bell) and NL (newline) characters would be displayed as "^G" and "^J" respectively. The most obvious disadvantage of this technique is that it impinges on available display space. In addition, such codes can be awkward to recognize, particularly when several are presented in close proximity. However, the number of control characters displayed is dramatically reduced when line buffering is used, because the predictive mechanism never encounters the editing characters typed when correcting individual lines.

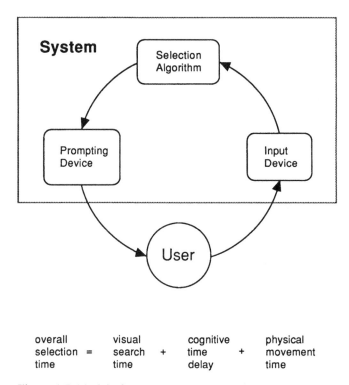

$$\begin{array}{lcl} \text{overall} & & \text{visual} & & \text{cognitive} & & \text{physical} \\ \text{selection} & = & \text{search} & + & \text{time} & + & \text{movement} \\ \text{time} & & \text{time} & & \text{delay} & & \text{time} \end{array}$$

Figure 4.5. Model of menu selection. After Gibler and Childress (1982).

RK-Pointer operates in an environment that includes only three nonprinting characters: SPACE, TAB, and NL. These are made visible in the menu by special symbols, although their display can be turned off if it proves distracting to the user.

4.4. Selecting from the menu

RK-Button has five special keys associated with item selection: a previous and next key to step through options, and three accept keys for entering predicted characters, words, and lines (see Table 4.2). RK-Pointer displays many menu items and allows the user to select both a menu item and a point within it (see Figure 4.3).

Figure 4.5 shows a model of menu selection performance that has been applied to severely disabled users of scanning aids. The time to select an element from a prompting display is expressed as the sum of three components: visual search time, cognitive time delay, and movement time. For individuals with more severe motor impairments, movement time dominates the text-generation rate.

Predictive text generation decreases the physical load on the user by increasing the cognitive load. Although cognitive time is often ignored, it is certainly useful to minimize the cognitive complexity and visual search time involved in selecting an item. Factors such as feedback to the user and display format can have a large impact on overall performance. The RK-Button and RK-Pointer interfaces have been engineered to provide, wherever possible, selection feedback at the point where the text will be entered.

When a menu selection is made, three things happen immediately: The context that constitutes short-term memory is updated; a new set of menu items is generated from long-term memory; and the new items are displayed. Furthermore, long-term memory must also be updated. It is helpful to avoid contaminating long-term memory if the text that has been entered contains errors. The Reactive Keyboard incorporates line-editing functions and delays long-term memory updates until after the newline character is selected. This means that errors that are corrected before the line is completed do not affect long-term memory. Although it may be difficult to erase errors from long-term memory once they have been made, the frequency-based prediction algorithm ensures that they do not reappear as likely predictions.

4.5. Metadialog

Only part of a user's interaction with the Reactive Keyboard concerns the actual selection of predictions. Several factors directly affect the nature of the text generation process but have more to do with controlling the medium than with the text message itself.

Table 4.2 divides the user's interaction with the Reactive Keyboard into six main categories:

selection control
display control
model control
error control
panic control
external model manipulation

Selection control is the main dialog component when interacting with the Reactive Keyboard. It concerns the actual selection of predictions, as discussed previously. All other categories constitute metadialog or tasks secondary to actual predictive text generation.

Table 4.4 shows how these categories of interaction are implemented in each of the three versions. The function names given in the table differ slightly from system to system. Also, only those features common to all systems are included. For RK-UNIX, functions can be bound to any key, except that some are command-line arguments that are specified when the system is invoked. For RK-PC, key assignments are fixed and are shown in typewriter font in the table – the remaining entries must be redefined using a special SETUP program. (Although not shown in the

Table 4.4. *Functional equivalents in the three implementations*

	RK-UNIX	RK-PC	RK-MAC

Selection control	Accept forward char
	Accept forward word
	Accept to end of line
	Previous prediction
	Next prediction
		`Arrow Right`
		`Insert`
		
		`End`
		
		`Page Up`
		`Page Down`
			Mouse-based menu item selection

Display control	Prediction length Prediction mode Show newlines Truncate at newlines	Prediction length Prediction mode Show newlines	Window functions control item and menu length Show newlines Truncate at newlines
Model control	Prime from file Zero-frequency file Model order Max frequency count Max memory Number to prime	Prime from file Zero-frequency file Model order Max frequency count Max memory Number to prime	Prime from file Zero-frequency file Model order Max frequency count Max memory Number to prime

Error control	Beginning of line
	End of line
	Backward character
	Forward character
	Delete character
	Backspace character
	Discard rest of line
	Previous line
	Next line
		`Home`
		`End`
		`Arrow Left`
		`Arrow Right`
		`Delete`
		`Backspace`
		`Escape`
		`Arrow Up`
		`Arrow Down`
			Standard text editing functions – cut, paste, delete, etc.

Panic control	Help Show key bindings Show arguments	Help (`F1`)	Scrollable on-line help document
External model manipulation	Modify priming file Create zero-frequency table Truncate prime file	Modify priming file Create zero-frequency table Truncate prime file	Modify priming file Create zero-frequency table

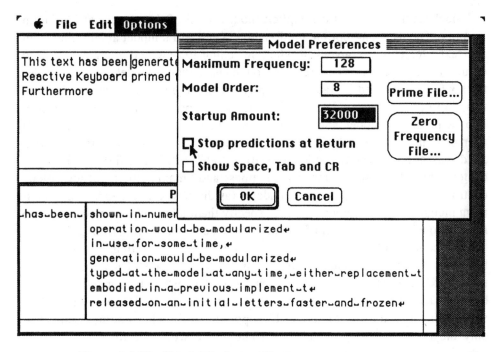

Figure 4.6. The "Model Preferences" menu.

table, control character alternatives – which are consistent with the UNIX defaults – are provided for many of these functions; see Appendix B.) For RK-MAC, most of the parameters are specified using the dialog box shown in Figure 4.6, which is obtained by selecting "Model Preferences" from the Options menu.

Display control is the means whereby users modify the parameters of the prompting device, whereas model control is the means whereby they modify the content of the model itself. Both of these metadialog components are forms of "explicit modeling": They give users control over the interaction environment. They are available in both RK-Button and RK-Pointer.

Display control has been discussed above in terms of how the user can set the length of predictions and determine how nonprinting characters are displayed. Table 4.4 shows four parameters that are used to control the display. (In fact, RK-UNIX has several more.) "Prediction length" and "prediction mode" determine the length of predictions and whether they are displayed on the screen or not. "Show newlines" and "truncate at newlines" determine whether the newline character is displayed and whether predictions stop when this character occurs. In RK-MAC the first two are controlled by varying the size of the prediction window, while the others are set from the menu shown in Figure 4.6 by clicking the boxes "Stop predictions at Return" and "Show Space, Tab and CR."

Model control concerns the explicit modification of the content of long-term memory. The user can reprime the Reactive Keyboard's model at any time from any text file. This is convenient when switching to new text entry contexts, to ensure that the predictions are relevant to the task at hand. Model control includes the six functions listed in Table 4.4, which are common to all versions. The first two, "prime from file" and "zero-frequency file," specify default files to be read into the predictive model when the program is invoked. The latter gives all ASCII characters in the order of their expected frequency of appearance in text (Section 5.2 discusses how this information is used). "Model order" specifies the number of context characters used to make predictions, and "maximum frequency count" controls the rate at which the model adapts (as discussed in Section 5.4). "Maximum memory" and "number to prime" specify the total amount of memory to use for the model and the number of characters to read when priming from a file.

Error control in RK-Button takes the form of line buffer editing. The process of text generation involves much more than simply entering text. Only about 50% of typical text editing keystrokes are for text entry – the rest are for cursor movement, deletion, and miscellaneous editing control functions. RK-Button isolates line editing functions at its user interface by supplying explicit line editing commands; only the finished text is modeled. An alternative would be to model all user behavior, including cursor movement and deletion, in an effort to provide greater text generation assistance. Both approaches have merits and drawbacks, which will be discussed in Chapter 5.

Error control in RK-Pointer is simpler and uses a standard point-and-click paradigm. In addition, the user can select text from the context area of the predictions window to erase previously entered characters. As with RK-Button, only the finished text is modeled, and it is incorporated into the model at the completion of each line.

By "panic control" we mean the provision of ways for the user to get help about using the interface. Apparently this type of system is easily understood and used after receiving brief introductory instructions – recall from Section 3.3 that the "help" key available to subjects in the Predict pilot experiment was *never* used. Nevertheless, both RK-Button and RK-Pointer include online help facilities listing available commands and their functions. In the case of RK-Button, most of these are related to line buffer editing.

The final category, external model manipulation, concerns tasks that are performed outside the Reactive Keyboard to customize its predictions to the user's text entry environment. These include modifying the priming file by explicitly editing it, and altering the standard zero-frequency table to correspond to the alphabet actually being used (see Chapter 5). A significant feature of the Reactive Keyboard is that the user can change the system's model completely by repriming it with a new file. This has an effect on predictions that is easy for users to understand even if they are unfamiliar with the precise mechanism of prediction.

4.6. Selection strategies

In most situations there are several different strategies that can be adopted for entering text using the Reactive Keyboard. First and foremost, the user must decide whether to type characters or look for predictions to select. In the latter case, there are often different ways of accepting the predictions.

For example, suppose a word is predicted and the user wants its root, but with a different suffix. With RK-Pointer, the user simply selects the correctly predicted text. This causes the menu to change. If the suffix, or even just its first letter, appears on the first page of the new menu, the user will probably want to select it. If not, the user may prefer to type it explicitly rather than seek it on later menu pages. Once the first letter of the suffix is typed, it is quite likely that the remainder of it will be predicted in full.

With RK-Button, various different strategies are available depending on the number of correct letters to be accepted. Suppose the user wants to enter the word "THESE," and "THEIR" is being predicted. Reasonable options are: first, to select the whole word and backspace twice (the keying sequence using the key bindings given in Appendix A is ^G^?^?), and second, to accept three characters individually (^A^A^A). A third option is available in the UNIX implementation of RK-Button, which has a repeat facility (called "increment factor," ^U) that repeats any command a multiple of four times. By using this, three characters may be accepted by first accepting four and then erasing one (^U^A^?).

In contrast to typing the letters directly, these strategies make use of only one, two, or three closely grouped function keys. The method of choice will depend on how easy it is for the user to switch between physically separated keys. Able-bodied readers may not immediately appreciate the time and energy required by some disabled users to switch between keys – even ones that are adjacent on the keyboard. Longer examples will of course present more interesting trade-offs between these three entry methods, as will examples involving lines comprising several words rather than words comprising several characters.

Returning to the example, once the prefix "THE" has been entered using RK-Button there are two ways of extending it into "THEIR." First, alternative predictions may be requested until the correct ending is displayed. Second, users may begin typing the desired next characters, "I" and then "R," possibly finishing the word by accepting the correct completion if it appears after the first character is typed. The choice between typing and looking for alternative predictions will often be based on knowledge of what has been typed previously and how likely it is that the desired completion will appear. While this may sound complicated, it becomes second nature with regular use of the Reactive Keyboard.

4.7. Further Reading

The concept of the Reactive Keyboard was first proposed by Witten et al. (1983). (Perhaps the name was unconsciously plagiarized from Mooers's (1966) "reactive typewriter," though actually this is completely unrelated, and referred to an ordinary time-sharing computer terminal!) Darragh et al. (1990) describe the Apple Macintosh interface, while Darragh (1988) and Darragh and Witten (1991) give a comprehensive account of the system and the background to its development.

The "magic number" seven plus or minus two is Miller's (1956) commonly used estimate of the number of items that can be retained in human short-term memory. Salthouse (1984) observes that a minimum preview size of seven letters is required for efficient copy-typing by normal subjects. Damerau (1971) investigates the relationship between grammatical correctness and both the model order and the length of predictions.

Dunn-Rankin (1978) studies how word discrimination in adult readers depends on the visual cues they are given – word length, prefixes, and so on. Nooteboom's (1981) research indicates that word beginnings may be less redundant than word endings, and that they provide strong visual cues to word recognition. However, Carlson et al. (1985) later found the reverse to be true – the ends of words being better predictors than their beginnings. To some extent this effect appears to be language-dependent.

5

The prediction mechanism

We have carefully separated the Reactive Keyboard's prediction mechanism from its user interface. As has already been noted, the same prediction mechanism can be accessed through quite different interfaces to give systems with a completely different "look and feel." This separation is particularly appropriate when dealing with tools for disabled people because different disabilities call for different physical interface mechanisms.

One of Predict's major shortcomings was its reliance on a fixed-length model that is often unable to make predictions because of incomplete k-tuple statistics. There is a conflict in assigning a value to k: On the one hand it should be large, because more specific predictions are likely to be more accurate, but on the other hand it should be small, to maximize the chance that the current context has been seen before so that at least some predictions are available.

The Reactive Keyboard seeks the best of both worlds by employing a variable-length context matching technique, which was originally developed to estimate character probabilities for text compression. Variable-length modeling proves extremely effective because it is capable of predicting from more complete lower-order models if less complete higher-order models fail to contain an instance of the current context. Matching variable-length contexts introduces a refinement to the short- and long-term memory structures presented in Chapter 2. Both now implicitly contain foreshortened contexts for partial matching that allow progressively shorter contexts to be used to locate possible continuations.

Variable-length models use a tree structure very similar to that described in Chapter 2 for the Dynamic Matrix (Figure 2.5). Instead of storing words in the tree, they store all k-tuples of length one up to some maximum, typically seven or eight. K-tuples of length one are, of course, individual characters; longer k-tuples may be partial or complete words or short phrases. All lower-order models are implicit in the highest-order model, so no extra storage is required.

5.1. Model construction

The model is stored in a tree structure that allows partial matches between the context and the model to be found economically. An example tree is shown in Figure 5.1a. Here, the phrase "to be or not t" is represented as a tree with maximum depth four (i.e., the value of k is 4). The children of the root – space ("#"), B, E, N, O, R, and T – are all the characters that have been seen in the null context, that is, all characters that have occurred. The children of the # that roots the leftmost subtree – B, N, O, and T – are characters that have occurred in the context #, that is,

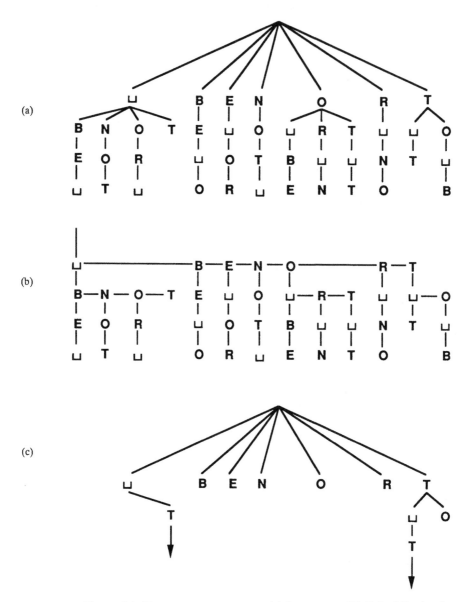

Figure 5.1. Tree memory structure: (a) in concept, (b) linked-list implementation, and (c) generating a prediction.

at the beginning of a word. The child of the leftmost B, namely E, is the only character that has occurred in the context #B, and its child # is the only one that has occurred in the context #BE. The tree is rather a stringy one because the sample of text is very small.

The aim of the storage structure is to allow predictions associated with sub-strings of the current context to be found quickly. A tree-structured scheme is essential to avoid repeated searches for each different context length. Figure 5.1b shows one way of storing the tree, where alternatives at each level are linked together as a list. Each node has four parts: a character element label, a frequency counter (not shown), a pointer to the next alternative at its level, and a pointer to the first element for this context at the level below. Alternatives at any level are listed alphabetically for presentation purposes only – frequency order is used in practice to speed updating and menu generation.

Models can become quite large and the tree structure needs to be carefully organized because of the real-time search and update requirements imposed by an interactive user interface. Moreover, the system needs to work continuously, with no upper bound to the amount of text that can be accommodated. These issues are taken up in Sections 5.3 and 5.4.

5.2. Model use

We now look at how the Reactive Keyboard's memory is used to generate its two-dimensional prompting display. The full 128-character ASCII alphabet is used, so that the user can enter all characters, including control characters, and 128 menu items are generated at each step. Menu creation is complicated by the possibility that some characters may not have occurred yet in the input stream and are therefore not represented in long-term memory.

Generating the menu items

The purpose of the model is to support prediction. Figure 5.1c shows the relevant part of the tree when predicting the character that follows the phrase "to be or not t." The prediction context is T#T. There are no predictions at this level (right arrow); neither are there any for the shortened context #T (left arrow). When the context is further truncated to T alone, two predictions – # and O – appear in the rightmost subtree; truncation to the null string generates seven – #, B, E, N, O, R, and T.

The Reactive Keyboard generates the initial characters of its predictions using a simple ordering strategy that favors longer contexts. First, any matches found for the highest-order context are added to the menu, starting with the most popular. Then, progressively shorter matches are made and any new character predictions that have not yet been encountered are added to the list, again in frequency order. This ensures that each initial menu character is unique and limits the total number of items to the size of the ASCII alphabet. When the context length becomes zero,

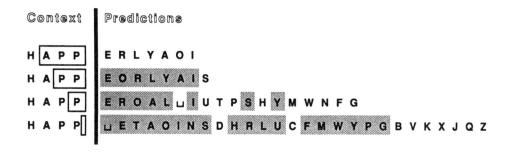

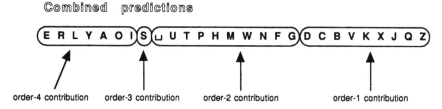

Figure 5.2. Generating initial letters for the menu. Based on a table in
Foulds et al. (1975).

all remaining characters not yet found but which have occurred in the input stream
are added in frequency order. Finally, all remaining characters that are not represented in the model – the ones with "zero frequency" – are added to the list.

For each of these 128 initial character predictions, concatenated predictions are
constructed by assuming that each newly predicted character is correct, shifting the
context to include it, and generating a further prediction. The effect is to follow
"into the future" a single path for every initial character. At each stage the most
popular alternative, that is, the one that has occurred most often in the past, is
chosen. This technique for concatenating predictions was first used in Predict, but
the Reactive Keyboard differs in that it bases predictions on frequency rather than
recency of occurrence.

Figure 5.2 gives an example of how the initial letters of predictions would be
generated if the user were spelling the word HAPPY and had already entered
HAPP. It is based on a 26-letter alphabet plus space, with $k = 4$. The alternative
predictions for each context length are shown in frequency order from left to right.
Notice that the relative popularity of candidate letters varies with the length of the
context used for prediction – for example, with three letters of context the most
popular predictions are E, R, L, . . . , in that order; while with no context they are #,
E, T, A, ... Once a letter appears at a given level it reappears at all lower levels
too, and these occurrences are grayed out in the figure because they do not
represent new contributions to the set of predictions. Letters not previously encoun-

tered at higher levels are added to the menu list in frequency order. The final set of predictions, combining all contributions from the various levels, is shown in order at the bottom of the figure.

Once the list of initial letters has been generated, each in turn is followed into the future to complete the menu item. Progressively longer concatenations are made by assuming that the current prediction is correct and destined to be accepted. In the present example, the prediction context APP would be shifted forward to make concatenated predictions. The process repeats with the projected new context until either the end-of-line character is predicted or the window width is exceeded. For example, if the current context APP predicted the initial letter Y, then Y would be assumed correct and the context shifted to PPY. This would be used to predict another letter, say #, and the process repeated with the projected context PY#. At this point, the concatenation Y# would be displayed for selection. In practice, further characters would probably be predicted as well, to complete the current menu item.

The zero-frequency problem

The zero-frequency problem was not encountered in the example of Figure 5.2 because the symbol set was restricted to the English alphabet. However, the Reactive Keyboard uses the complete ASCII character set as prediction elements, and many of these never or only rarely occur in normal text generation. Examination of several fairly large text files – both English and program source code – revealed that approximately 30 to 40 ASCII characters were not represented at all. Moreover, whenever memory starts unprimed, even commonly used symbols initially have no frequency listing in the model. For example, only the letters #, B, E, N, O, R, and T are contained in the unprimed model in Figure 5.1; all other symbols have zero frequency so far.

The Reactive Keyboard deals with the zero-frequency problem by reading a standard, or user-defined, zero-frequency table before starting a session. This contains a frequency-ordered list of the entire symbol set derived from a large sample of "representative" text. It is assumed that the text sample used will contain instances of most of the low frequency characters that the user would need to generate. The table is used to build a backup zero-frequency level into the model that is scanned after the adaptive part of long-term memory. This is equivalent to adding a $k = 0$ level to the model. Any symbols with equal frequency are listed in the table in collating order. Symbols that do not occur in the source sample will have a count of zero and are therefore presented last in ASCII sequence.

If necessary, users can explicitly modify or replace the zero-frequency table. For example, one could place zero-frequency symbols that cannot possibly occur after zero-frequency symbols that might occur, but that are not represented in the table's source data. The zero-frequency symbols could also be sorted by type and listed in a likely order such as white space followed by lower-case alphabetic, upper-case alphabetic, punctuation, numbers, control codes, and finally other nonprinting characters. Ideally the frequency table would be automatically coupled to the global context currently in use.

5.3. Model size and content

The success of a variable-length model depends on four main factors that characterize both the local context, or short-term memory, and the global context, or long-term memory:

the type of elements from which k-tuples are composed

the maximum order k of the model

the model size, measured as the total number of k-tuples used

the nature of the text incorporated into the model

We have already seen that the Reactive Keyboard uses single-character k-tuple elements and k-tuple lengths whose order varies between one and a preset maximum, typically seven or eight. We now examine how the last two factors – size and content – are handled.

Long-term memory size

It is difficult to estimate accurately the minimum size needed to store a complete model of an open-ended stream of text. If s is the size of the alphabet ($s = 128$ for ASCII), then the theoretical lower and upper bounds for a complete model of maximum length k are $s + k$ and $s + \Sigma_{i=1}^{k} s^i$ nodes respectively. The lower bound is for the unlikely case of a continuous stream of a single character, plus room for the zero-frequency table. The upper bound is unrealistically high as most of the possible higher-order k-tuples never occur in practice. For example, a half million character sample of English text was found to need only 150,000 of the possible 34,630,287,616 nodes to store a complete model – less than 0.0005% ($s = 128$, $k = 5$).

Another approach is to define the *type-token ratio* of a sample of text as the ratio of the number of different words (i.e., "types") to the total number of words in it (i.e., "tokens"). The ratio is expected to fall as progressively larger text samples are considered, because fewer new words are encountered. It may be possible to set a reasonable upper bound on model size by deriving a theoretical type-token function to fit observed k-tuple data closely, and then to extrapolate an asymptotic value for the total number of unique k-tuples in an infinite sample. Although some attempts to do so have been reported, the results obtained are generally rather inconclusive.

A better feel for the maximum size encountered in practice can be gained by examining large representative text samples. Results of text compression experiments and experience using the Reactive Keyboard suggest that between 100,000 and 200,000 nodes are required to model enough text to make accurate predictions when $k \leq 7$.

Practical limits are imposed on the number of nodes by implementation considerations such as the amount of storage space available, the size of each tree node, and the type of data storage employed. Restricting memory size raises the specter of running out of space before the model is complete. When it is full, further new k-tuples can be ignored – and only those already in the model used – or some mechanism for *forgetting* less useful k-tuples can be used. These will be discussed shortly.

Priming and representative text

By far the most important factor affecting long-term memory content is the actual text used to prime the model. Finding truly representative text samples can be difficult as the statistical characteristics of seemingly similar samples can vary greatly. This implies that the text sample used for priming must be carefully selected to be as representative as possible of what the user wants to generate.

The Reactive Keyboard derives its model in three ways, using a combination of automatic and explicit modeling techniques. Priming occurs

automatically from a default, or user-defined, start-up file

automatically from current user inputs

explicitly from any text file the user adds into the model

Automatic modeling keeps long-term memory up to date, yet the user has the option of explicitly specifying, augmenting, or altering the text used to prime it.

The way in which priming files are maintained differs slightly between versions of the Reactive Keyboard, to suit the environment in which they run. For example, in the UNIX implementation the default start-up text file is a log file of all text generated to date by the user (although any text file could be used). After priming with the start-up file, the initial model and the log file are automatically updated as new text is generated. If necessary, any entry errors stored in the log file can be corrected by editing the file. This is easy to do using a standard text editor, because the log file comprises a plain textual record of all input.

Global context control is available during a session through explicit priming from any text file. This feature also allows long-term memory to serve as a store in which the user may capture program output – such as a list of filenames – on a temporary basis, for possible future use in text generation use. Moreover, in RK-MAC long-term memory can be erased before priming, giving the user the option of keeping multiple contexts concurrently in the model, or – by first clearing it – switching between separate, possibly very different, global contexts. Other than the default log file, all text files used for priming are explicitly selected by the user.

User behavior

The next factor affecting model content involves a choice of whether to model user behavior in its entirety, including input line editing and control functions, or to isolate these user interface tasks and only model the finished text. Experiments have shown that when able-bodied knowledge workers use various text editors to create documents, and when secretaries use editors to transcribe and update documents, only about one-half of the keystrokes are for text entry. Another quarter are for cursor movement, an eighth for deletion, and the rest for miscellaneous functions. These results suggest that it may not be sufficient just to model the final form of the text generated if maximal predictive assistance is to be provided.

Predictive text generation systems usually base their canonical communication models on representative samples of completed text rather than on the user's actual behavior. Whether this is appropriate depends on the environment in which text is being generated. Modeling all behavior gives extra help with nontext tasks, but predictability is reduced by sprinkling less redundant, less predictable, edit and control operators among what would otherwise be connected text. Prediction and display of nontext operators can also be problematic and could unduly clutter the prompting display.

The main advantage of modeling only finished text is its simplicity. Long-term memory is uncluttered and user typing errors are filtered out at the user interface. The best approach for a specific user depends on the application and the user's individual ability and circumstances. It may be possible to construct separate text and edit task memories in order to get the best of both worlds. However, current versions of the Reactive Keyboard model only the finished text.

Special tokens

Just as it is possible to exclude certain user behavior from the model, special elements can be added to it that do not occur in the input stream but which nevertheless serve to guide predictions. An example might be a distinctive character inserted to mark the beginning or end of each text generation session, for later use when initializing the context at the start of a new session before any new user-generated context is available. This assumes that users will generate predictable command sequences when logging out and logging in – such as reading new electronic mail.

Although we have restricted attention to character-based models, other element types and node labels are possible. These could be linguistic elements such as Predict's words and strings, or specialized tokens that represent a class of lexical items such as dates or telephone numbers. The memory structure could be made more task-specific by parsing the input into larger tokens in an effort to increase the accuracy of predictions, but as a consequence this would greatly reduce the generality of the system.

5.4. Model maintenance

Three operations are required to update and maintain the model: adding new k-tuples to the model as new input behavior is experienced, incrementing frequency counts of recurring k-tuples, and removing old k-tuples to make way for new ones when the model is full.

The update procedure processes each input character as follows. First, if memory is full, nodes are deleted to ensure that enough space is available for possible additions. Then, at each level of the tree, the part of it associated with the current context is searched for the input character. If found, the corresponding node's occurrence count is incremented and frequency order is maintained by re-sorting the list of alternatives. Otherwise, a new node is created and added to the end of the list with a count of one.

Frequency counts

It is convenient to represent frequency counts as fixed-length integers, in which case the possibility of overflow must be considered. The Reactive Keyboard simply halves frequency counts just before overflow. All associated counts at the current level are also halved. Some accuracy is lost, but the relative frequency of alternatives and the ability to discriminate between them is maintained. Any divisor greater than one could be used to reduce counts; two works well in practice and is efficiently implemented as a bit-shift operation.

Whatever divisor is chosen, special attention must be given to nodes whose frequency counts fall to zero. Such nodes could either be retained by restoring their counts to one, or deleted and the space freed for subsequent new nodes. It is possible to do both by restoring nodes when space is available and forgetting them (and their subtrees) when memory is full. Frequency-count reduction can therefore conveniently double as a simple "forgetting" algorithm.

Frequency reduction creates a sort of memory "blurring" even when nodes are not deleted. The statistical significance of a k-tuple slowly decreases if it is used infrequently relative to other alternatives, ensuring that unrepresentative statistics, caused perhaps by a change in the kind of text being generated, cannot influence prediction efficiency forever.

Text compression experiments have been performed to determine an optimal frequency count size. Larger counts retain probability distributions to higher accuracy, but increase the time constant for "forgetting." It was encouraging to discover that when the number of bits used for frequency counts was reduced to six or eight for storage reasons, the model actually performed better than earlier versions using 32-bit counts. This surprisingly low value indicates that sensitivity to drift in the statistics of the text is more important than accurate representation of the probability distributions. It is quite acceptable to store counts in 8-bit bytes. Of course this increased sensitivity and space saving comes at the price of doubling the number of frequency reductions required for every bit by which the count is decreased.

Forgetting

Because the Reactive Keyboard's store is finite – and possibly insufficient – exceptional action must be taken if and when it becomes full. If the system is to continue adapting, less useful k-tuples must be forgotten to make room for new ones as they occur. This process, known as *forgetting,* can take several forms, one of which is the memory blurring caused by the finite resolution of frequency counts discussed earlier. It seems clear that in a changing environment it is desirable to allow old traces that no longer occur to be replaced by new ones. Indeed, it may be that prediction efficiency depends as much on what the model forgets as on what it remembers.

Forgetting has two phases: selecting what to forget and then actually deleting it from long-term memory. Deletion is relatively simple once "forgettable" k-tuples are identified. The simplest scheme is to forget based on frequency of occurrence, as other automatic schemes would require a considerable amount of extra storage per node. The least frequently seen leaf nodes, which are presumably the least likely to recur, can be deleted from long-term memory when new space is required. Experiments have shown that this strategy is better than recency-based or random forgetting algorithms employing nodes of equivalent size. Moreover, when the store is full, the frequency halving algorithm can be altered to delete rather than restore nodes and subtrees whose frequencies have fallen to zero.

As well as keeping long-term memory within predefined limits, forgetting adds a degree of automatic error correction to the model. Because of their low frequency of occurrence, erroneous entries will be the first to be deleted.

Practical considerations

The ability to edit the log file manually provides a further degree of control over what is remembered and what is forgotten. Although it is rarely necessary to edit the log file to remove errors, there are two practical reasons to do so. They stem from the use of a frequency-based prediction heuristic. At times there may be a desire to override certain high-frequency items explicitly in favor of more recent, yet lower frequency, ones. One common example in the UNIX environment occurs when an electronic mail correspondent changes address. The frequency-based prediction heuristic will faithfully predict the old address instead of the new one until the latter has occurred more often than the former. All that is necessary to rectify the situation is to edit the log file and either delete occurrences of the old address or, better still, change them all to the new address, thus preserving the historical context. Such action is not strictly necessary since the new address will be predicted as an alternative to the old and will eventually preempt it. Editing the address simply forces the change and speeds future correspondence by making the correct address the first one offered.

The other reason to edit the log file is related to the amount of time it takes to prime the Reactive Keyboard when logging in to the host system. For example, in the UNIX implementation, once the log file has grown to around 50,000 characters the additional start-up delay becomes noticeable (of course the delay varies considerably with host system load). To alleviate this, all versions automatically read a predetermined number of characters from the end of the priming file, if it exceeds a certain length. Moreover, RK-UNIX and RK-PC have a facility for explicitly truncating the priming file. In the absence of an automatic truncation scheme, a recency-based forgetting strategy is achieved by simply deleting the beginning lines of the log file and reinitializing long-term memory. Truncation to 2,000 lines has worked well in practice as a reasonable compromise between retained context and start-up priming time, but this of course depends on the host system's speed. Despite the apparent awkwardness, the flexibility gained from having an explicitly editable log file has proved extremely useful.

5.5. Summary and further reading

The Reactive Keyboard combines and exploits many concepts of predictive text generation and has potential to provide better predictive assistance than has heretofore been possible. A useful distinction is made between the system's user interface and the underlying model it employs; this permits several different interface options and model implementations. Chapter 6 presents the details of implementing adaptive, tree-structured, variable-length long-term memory.

The variable-length tree structure was introduced by Cleary (1980) and implemented by Darragh et al. (1983), and was used to derive adaptive character probabilities for text compression by Cleary and Witten (1984). Bell et al. (1990) gives a comprehensive description of this and other text compression methods. A similar variable-length tree structure was used by Jones (1981) for the Dynamic Matrix discussed in Chapter 2. The data structure in Figure 5.1 is called a "trie" (from the word re*trie*val), and is covered in standard textbooks such as Standish (1980).

Theoretical models of empirically derived type-token ratios are discussed by Carroll (1966). Gibler (1981) examined various statistical measures for characterizing text samples and found that the statistics of seemingly similar samples can vary greatly. A standard corpus for this kind of study is described by Kucera and Francis (1967), who explicitly mention the high degree of variability and caution against assuming that the statistics are representative of English text in general. Further references to corpora for various languages can be found in Carlson et al. (1985), Cress (1986), and Hunnicutt (1987).

Whiteside et al. (1982) demonstrate that only a low proportion of keystrokes are actually used for text entry, and also present an "index of predictive association," which can be used for higher-level prediction of context switches – for example, from cursor movement to text entry and back.

6
Implementation

The Reactive Keyboard is a fairly complex program. In particular, the predictive part involves some intricate manipulation of pointers that warrants a fairly detailed description. In order to encourage it to be reimplemented on different systems and tailored for different users' circumstances, a complete description of the program code for the IBM PC is provided. The predictive part of the code is exactly the same for the UNIX and Macintosh versions; the PC version was chosen because of the simplicity of its user interface. Appendix C contains a listing of the program, in which the lines are numbered for reference in the text below. In addition, critical portions of the program are presented in the form of pseudocode as figures in this chapter, with numbers that point to corresponding lines in Appendix C. Complete documentation for the program is reproduced in Appendix B.

We begin with a review of the overall structure of the system and a survey of the routines it contains. Next the data structures are presented. The core of the system, and the most complex part, is the actual predictive mechanism. It is described and illustrated with an extended example of constructing the model, making predictions, and updating the model. The command-line interface is straightforward and needs little elaboration. A number of different trade-offs between time, space, and implementation complexity are implicit in the data structure chosen for the model. The final section here discusses some alternative data structures that may be worth considering for different implementation platforms.

6.1. Structure of the system

The overall program is divided into two parts: the command-line editor and the predictive code, which correspond to the topics discussed in Chapters 4 and 5 respectively. These two components reside in the files listed in Appendix C, rk_com.c and rk_pred.c. The main program is in rk_com.c and drives the entire system. The remaining routines in rk_com.c take care of updating the display and executing commands. Rk_pred.c handles all aspects that involve the model: its construction, use for prediction, and updating.

As the pseudocode in Figure 6.1 shows, the main program (lines 88–318) first prints a welcome message, and then performs some initialization that involves reading a file of set-up parameters and constructing the initial model. (Print statements are shown in bold so that they can be identified easily.) Next it enters a loop that processes keystrokes. At the beginning of the loop the MS-DOS prompt is displayed, a prediction is made and displayed, and a keystroke is awaited. Key-

```
main()

    print welcome message

    read_setup()
        • open parameter file (modified using SETUP)
        • read in parameters for model and display control

    construct_the_model()                                  see Figure 6.5

    loop until user quits the program:

        print user's prompt
        make_a_prediction()                                see Figure 6.7
        display_line()
            • print the command line and prediction

        wait for user input (a keystoke or function key)

        process user input as one of:
            accept predictions
            adjust model or display parameters
            ask for help
            edit the command line
            leave the program
            reprime the model
            execute_a_command()
                • send the completed command to DOS
                • update_the_model()                       see Figure 6.9
```

Figure 6.1. Pseudocode for the overall program.

strokes either control the selection of predictions or involve editing of the command line; these functions are described in the documentation reproduced in Appendix B.

Other than initial construction of the model, the only routines that involve the predictive portion of the code are make_a_prediction and update_the_model. The latter is called from execute_a_command to ensure that only completed, and presumably correct, command lines are used to update the model. Details of the predictive part of the code are given below.

Figure 6.2 relates the structure of the Reactive Keyboard to the communication-aid architecture introduced in Chapter 1 (Figure 1.4). The selection algorithm component is expanded to illustrate how the three main parts of the predictive code are connected to the prompting and input devices, and to long- and short-term memory. Construct_the_model reads the priming file and initializes the contents of both memories. Make_a_prediction uses the current context stored in short-term memory to access long-term memory, creates predictions, and displays them on the prompting device. Selections made with the input device, in

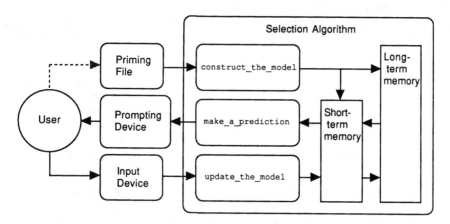

Figure 6.2. Overview of the system.

conjunction with the context in short-term memory, are used by `update_the_model` to modify long-term memory.

All the major subroutines are listed in Table 6.1, together with a brief comment on what they do. Routines that are called by a particular routine follow it in the list and are indented with chevrons. For example, `construct_the_model` calls `prime`, which calls `insert_char`. The list is divided into logically related groups of routines. The first three sections constitute the predictive code contained in `rk_pred.c`, whereas the final one is the command-line interface of `rk_com.c`. The routines appear in the same sequence in Appendix C. The only exception is `read_setup`, which appears at the end of `rk_pred.c` rather than in `rk_com.c` as Table 6.1 would imply.

6.2. Constants and data structures

Several compile-time constants are defined that set defaults for the Reactive Keyboard, improve the readability of the code, and facilitate easy modification. The top of Figure 6.3a reproduces the main constant definitions in `rk_com.c`, namely the number of command lines to retain as history and their maximum length; the maximum size of the character set; and the maximum size of string buffers used internally for storing command lines and so forth. Halfway down the figure appears the main constant definition in `rk_pred.c`, namely the maximum order of model (k) that can be accommodated. Other definitions that appear in the program include ASCII and PC-specific codes for interpreting keystrokes, the maximum size of directory names and filenames, and some display functions that use the ANSII display driver if it is present and standard DOS functions if it is not (lines 53–61 and 461–71 of Appendix C).

Table 6.1. *Names of routines and their locations in Appendix C*

Model construction	`construct_the_model`	539–587	Initialize and prime the model
	» `prime`	590–616	Prime the model
	» » `insert_char`	619–696	Insert current character into model in context k down to 1
	» » » `create_node`	699–721	Return a pointer to a new node
	» » » `show_progress`	724–740	Print a number to indicate progress when priming
Making predictions	`make_a_prediction`	743–769	Return pointer to the current prediction
	» `find_first_chars`	772–800	Find first characters of all predictions in context
	» `extend_pred`	803–826	Extend a prediction, given its initial character
	» » `find_char`	829–846	Scan the model for predictions, returning tree pointers
	» » `best_pred`	849–862	Return the single best prediction for this context
Updating the model	`update_the_model`	865–886	Incorporate a command line into the model
	» `insert_char`		(See above)
	» `log_to_file`	889–918	Save completed commands
	`prime_from_file`	921–942	Prime the model from a file
	» `prime`		(See above)
Command-line interface	`main`	88–318	Await and process input keystrokes
	» `read_setup`	943–979	Read setup parameters
	» `construct_the_model`		(See above)
	» `make_a_prediction`		(See above)
	» `display_line`	321–367	Display command and prediction
	» `execute_a_command`	370–392	Send a command line to DOS
	» » `update_the_model`		(See above)

a)
```
63.    #define MAX_HIST      8          Number of com_bufs to save
65.    #define MAX_SAVE     64          Length of each com_buf to save
66.    #define MAX_SET     128          Maximum number of symbols
67.    #define MAX_BUF     256          Maximum size of a text buffer

73.    int     x_position, y_position;  Starting position of the current line on the screen

75.    char    com_buf[MAX_BUF],                             Entered part of line
76.            * c_end,                                      End of comand line
77.            * current,                        Current position in command line
78.            prev_buf[MAX_HIST][MAX_SAVE];              Previous commands
79.    int     last_command,                      Index of last command saved
80.            t_last_command;                    Temporary version of above

82.    char    pred_buff[MAX_BUF];                          Prediction buffer
83.    int     pred_number;             Index of the current prediction in first[]


454.   #define MAX_K         10                   Maximum order of the model

)6-523. char   zero_freq[MAX_SET] = {                       Zero frequency table
508.           '\n',    ' ',    'e',    's',    't',    'r',    'a',    'l',
509.           'n',    '.',    'c',    'i',    'm',    'o',    'd',    'h',
...            . . .
523.           '\31',  '\32',  '\33',  '\34',  '\35',  '\36',  \37',  '\177'};

532.   char    first[MAX_SET],                 The first letter of each prediction
533.           curr_context[MAX_BUF],             Current context for prediction
534.           prev_context[MAX_K + 1],          To remember previous contexts
535.           last_chars[MAX_K + 1];             Last max_k chars put in model
```

(b)   prev_buf[][]:   first[]:   pred_buf[]:

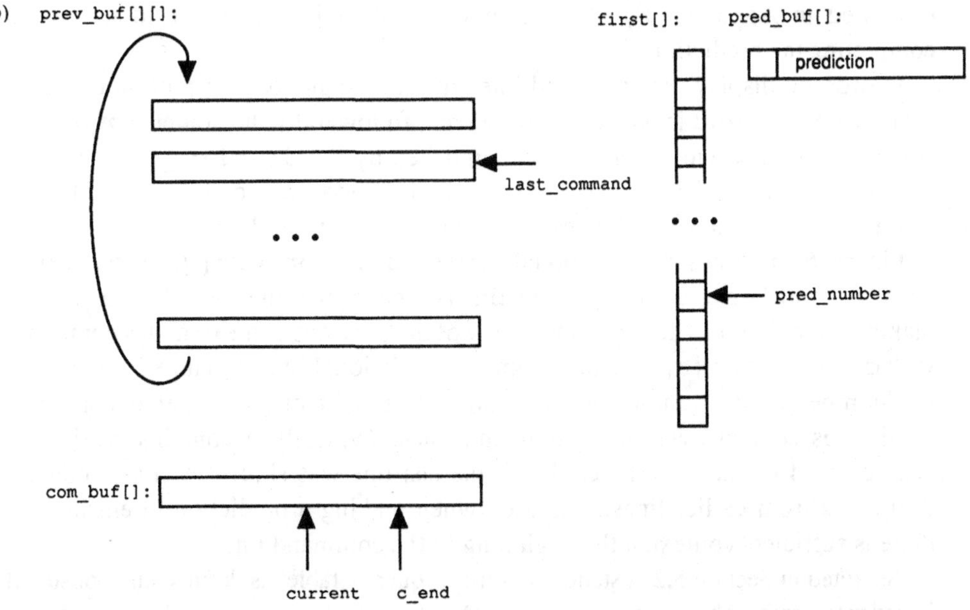

Figure 6.3. Storing commands and predictions: (a) C definitions and variables and (b) the data structures.

Each of the two files has its own data structure. The command-line editor's are simplest and are described first. Access is provided to previously entered commands through a circular list of buffers, prev_buf[ ][ ], each capable of holding a command line. Throughout this chapter we adopt the C language convention of using square brackets to indicate arrays, so prev_buf[ ][ ] is an array of arrays – in this case, an array of character strings. This data structure is defined at the top of Figure 6.3a and depicted in the left-hand part of Figure 6.3b. Last_command is used by the "previous-command" and "next-command" operations (bound to the Arrow Up and Arrow Down keys; see Appendix B) to move backward and forward through the history list. The current command line resides in com_buf[ ], shown underneath in Figure 6.3b. The end of the text entered is marked by c_end, and the current position of the cursor is pointed to by current. When execute_a_command is called with a completed command line, com_buf[ ] is copied to the current position in the history list, prev_buf[last_command+1][ ].

The data structure shown at the right of Figure 6.3b is associated with the predictive part of the code. The array first[ ] holds the initial character of each prediction for the current context, while pred_buf[ ] contains the most likely prediction. It is not actually necessary for all initial characters to be generated and stored, but it turns out to be convenient to do so. Only the most likely prediction is filled out to its full length. The first character of pred_buf[ ] is copied from the relevant item of the first[ ] array. Pred_number is changed by the previous- and next-prediction commands (bound to the Page Up and Page Down keys described in Appendix B) to indicate which item in first[ ] to use when completing the prediction.

In order to display the command line with the prediction, the portion of com_buf[ ] up to c_end is written to the screen, followed by the contents of pred_buf[ ] in inverse video. This is accomplished by the display_line routine (see below). The variables x_position and y_position at the top of Figure 6.3a record the screen coordinates of the start of the current line.

Figure 6.3a shows the additional arrays curr_context[ ], prev_context[ ], and last_chars[ ]. The first is used to store the current context when making a prediction. The second is a copy of the previous context, and is compared with curr_context[ ] before making a prediction. If it has changed, the prediction number pred_number is set to zero. Last_chars[ ] is used to maintain a continuous context over short command lines. Typically it contains the final k characters of the last line typed, but if the last line was short it will also contain characters from earlier lines. It is used when making a prediction to ensure that there is sufficient context at the beginning of the command line.

As noted in Section 5.2, a standard "zero-frequency table" is defined and consulted in order to predict characters that have not been encountered before. These characters will be predicted in the order in which they appear in the table. The table is stored in

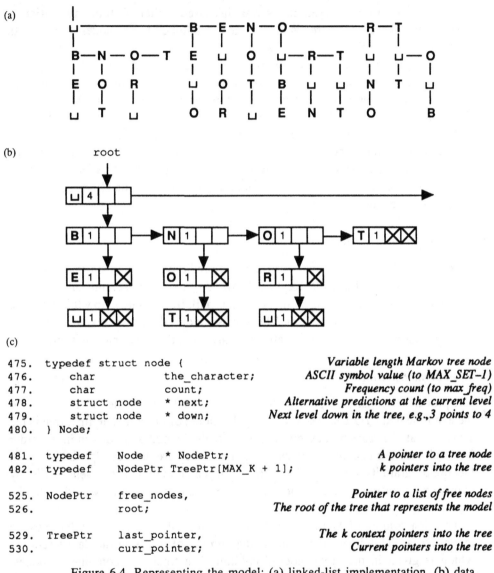

Figure 6.4. Representing the model: (a) linked-list implementation, (b) data structure, and (c) C definition of the data structure.

the array `zero_freq[]` in Figure 6.3a (see Appendix C for the full table). The UNIX and Macintosh versions permit the zero-frequency table to be defined by the user, but the IBM PC version does not, although the table can of course be altered by editing the code.

Section 5.1 discussed how the model is stored in a tree structure that allows partial matches between the context and the model to be found quickly. Figure 6.4b shows the actual storage method for the leftmost part of the tree of Figure 6.4a, the same "to be or not to t" example as was discussed earlier. Within any particular context, each level of the tree is represented as a linked list of nodes. A node has four components: the character that it represents, the occurrence count of this character in the present context, a pointer to the next level down in the tree, and a pointer to the next alternative prediction at this level. In the figure, the arrows are pointers and the crossed boxes represent null pointers. Figure 6.4c defines the node data type (Node), and creates type definitions for a pointer to a node (NodePtr) and for an array of k node pointers (TreePtr), one for each context length. Also defined is a pointer to the root of the tree (root), and two TreePtr arrays with k node pointers each. The purpose of these will be described shortly. Finally a pointer to the free-space list (free_nodes) is defined; space will be allocated dynamically when execution begins.

6.3. The predictive core

This section describes the code for the basic predictive mechanism that underlies all versions of the Reactive Keyboard. We do this by presenting an extensive example that shows how long-term memory is built from scratch, how this structure is used to made a prediction, and how it is modified as new text is seen. The routines that implement this code are summarized in the upper part of Table 6.1.

Model construction

The process of constructing, or "priming," the model is illustrated in Table 6.2 for the example text "TO BE OR NOT T" and a model of order 4. The final tree is the same as that of Figure 6.3, except that in the table the nodes are drawn in the order in which they are inserted whereas in the figure they are ordered alphabetically. In fact the program itself uses neither of these; instead it maintains frequency order by dynamically sorting the tree as nodes are inserted. This, however, would make the example more difficult to follow.

The first column of Table 6.2 shows the number of characters inserted into the model so far. This is not the same as the number of nodes in the data structure, which is given in the "total nodes" column. The final tree contains 43 nodes, representing 14 characters of text. The second column shows the context in which the current character is being inserted, followed by the current character and the level in the tree (1, 2, 3, or 4) to which the rest of the row pertains. For example, character number 4 is a B, and occurs in the context TO#. The next column, entitled "insert_char reports," contains a record of the updates made to the tree, whereas the final column shows the structure of long-term memory after the insertion of each character. The uneven spacing of the tree at the beginning is merely to leave room in the picture for subsequent insertions.

Table 6.2 was generated by inserting print statements into the construct_ the_model and insert_char routines. Figure 6.5 gives pseudocode for these,

Table 6.2. *Example of building the model*

	Context	Level	insert_char reports	Total nodes	Long-term memory
1		T : 4	Null level ptr	0	
		: 3	Null level ptr		
		: 2	Null level ptr		
		: 1	Start added T	1	
2		O : 4	Null level ptr	1	
		: 3	Null level ptr		
	T	: 2	Start added O	2	
		: 1	T, end added O	3	
3		# : 4	Null level ptr	3	
	TO	: 3	Start added #	4	
	O	: 2	Start added #	5	
		: 1	T,O, end added #	6	
4	TO#	B : 4	Start added B	7	
	O#	: 3	Start added B	8	
	#	: 2	Start added B	9	
		: 1	T,O,#, end added B	10	
5	O#B	E : 4	Start added E	11	
	#B	: 3	Start added E	12	
	B	: 2	Start added E	13	
		: 1	T,O,#,B, end added E	14	
6	#BE	# : 4	Start added #	15	
	BE	: 3	Start added #	16	
	E	: 2	Start added #	17	
		: 1	T,O, Found		
7	BE#	O : 4	Start added O	18	
	E#	: 3	Start added O	19	
	#	: 2	B, end added O	20	
		: 1	T, Found		

Table 6.2. *(cont.)*

	Context	Level	insert_char reports	Total nodes	Long-term memory
8	E#O	R : 4	Start added R	21	
	#O	: 3	Start added R	23	
	O	: 2	#, end added R	24	
		: 1	T,O,#,B,E, end added R		
9	#OR	# : 4	Start added #	25	
	OR	: 3	Start added #	26	
	R	: 2	Start added #	27	
		: 1	T,O, Found		
10	OR#	N : 4	Start added N	28	
	R#	: 3	Start added N	29	
	#	: 2	B,O, end added N	30	
		: 1	T,O,#,B,E,R, end added N	31	
11	R#N	O : 4	Start added O	32	
	#N	: 3	Start added O	33	
	N	: 2	Start added O	34	
		: 1	T, Found		
12	#NO	T : 4	Start added T	35	
	NO	: 3	Start added T	36	
	O	: 2	#,R, end added T	37	
		: 1	Found		
13	NOT	# : 4	Start added #	38	
	OT	: 3	Start added #	39	
	T	: 2	O, end added #	40	
		: 1	T,O, Found		
14	OT#	T : 4	Start added T	41	
	T#	: 3	Start added T	42	
	#	: 2	B,O,N, end added T	43	
		: 1	Found		

```
541-587.  construct_the_model()                    Initialize and prime the model

548-558.      allocate model memory
559-564.      set up root node and tree_pointer[] array
565-572.      read zero-frequency file if one exists
573-576.      prime(priming_file, last_pointer)
577-583.      initialize context[] buffer to the last few chars of priming_file
584-587.      prepare to make initial predictions


592-616.  prime(file, tree_pointer)              Prime the model with characters from a file

600-607.      find place in file to start priming from
608-609.      print starting priming message

  610.          for each character                        Construct the model
  ---               print character_number
  611.              for level = k downto 1           Update memory from current symbol
  ---                   if level == k then
  ---                       print context, character, ":", level
  ---                   else  print context, " :", level
  612.                  tree_pointer[level] =
                          insert_char(tree_pointer[level-1], character)
  613.              after every 100 characters are read
  614.                  show_progress()        Print how many more characters to prime
615-616.      print done priming message


621-696.  insert_char(current_level_pointer,      Insert current character into the model
                      the_character)

  632.          if current_level_pointer == NULL then    No predictions at this level
  ---               print Null level ptr
  633.              current_pointer = NULL
  634.              goto exit
  635.
636-637.      current_pointer = current_level_pointer->down
638-641.      if current_pointer != NULL then    Check the current level's "down" pointer
642-662.          while the character is not found  Scan linked list to find the character
  ---                 print current_pointer->the_character, ", "
  657.              current_pointer = current_pointer->next

663-665.      if the character was found
  ---               print Found
  673.          increment current_pointer->count
  674.          if current_pointer->count == max_freq
675-679.             halve all counts in this context at this level
(666-672)         re-sort this level of tree to maintain frequency order

680-684.      else
  ---               if at the start of the list print Start
  ---               else print end
  ---➤              print added, the_character
                                          Add a new node at this level of the tree
  685.          current_pointer               = create_node()
686-687.          current_pointer->the_character = the_character
  688.          current_pointer->count         = 1
  689.          current_pointer->next          = NULL
  689.          current_pointer->down          = NULL
690-693.          link new node into tree and set associated pointers

  694.  exit:
  ---       print newline
695-696.      return(current_pointer)
```

Figure 6.5. Pseudocode for model construction.

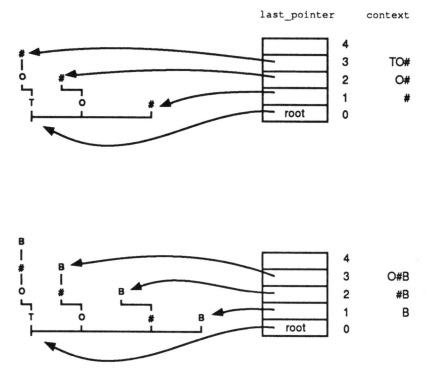

Figure 6.6. Examples of pointers into the tree.

and the code prints the entire table except for the final column of tree diagrams. Print statements are shown in bold so that they can be identified easily. The leftmost column gives the numbers of the lines in Appendix C that implement the individual pseudocode statements, where applicable.

`Construct_the_model` initializes and primes the model. First it allocates an initial amount of memory for the model, as specified by the `max_nodes` parameter. Then it reads the priming file and uses it to create the initial model. If the file contains more than `max_prime` characters, then the first part of the file is skipped so that only that number of characters are read. For each character read, a block of lines is printed, one for each level in the tree (see Table 6.2). The first line shows the character number, the current context, the character itself, and the highest level in the tree; subsequent lines give just context and level. For example (for character 4),

```
4    TO#  B  :4
      O#     :3
       #     :2
             :1
```

`Insert_char` is called to insert the character at the appropriate point in each level of the tree. During insertion of a character, the tree is accessed through pointers to the appropriate place at the current level. These tree pointers are collected in an array called `last_pointer[]`, and Figure 6.6 shows them before and after the update operation on character 4. The third element of the array points to the third level of the tree, and so on down to the zeroth element, which points to the root. The fourth element is never consulted, although it is set during the first iteration of the update loop (line 612 of Figure 6.5) to simplify the code. The `insert_char` routine scans for the current letter at the level *below* that given to it in the first parameter. It returns the position at which that character is found, or inserted. Consequently, after the update operation, the appropriate tree pointer from the previous level becomes the tree pointer for the current level, with the root pointer remaining constant.

The `insert_char` routine does one of four things. If the current level pointer is null, it simply prints that fact and returns. This only occurs at the beginning when the tree has levels that are completely empty, as Table 6.2 shows for the first three characters entered. Otherwise, the current level is scanned for the character. If it is found, its count is incremented and the list of alternatives at that level is re-sorted if necessary to maintain frequency order. If the character does not appear at that level, it is added to the end of the list. A special case occurs when the level is initially empty, in which case the character forms the start of the list. Either way, adding a node involves initializing all four of the node data structure components shown in Figure 6.4c. In each case, `insert_char` returns a pointer to the current character at that level, which `construct_the_model` places in the `last_pointer[]` array in readiness for processing the next character. The pseudocode for `insert_char` contains several print statements that were included to complete the trace shown in Table 6.2.

Table 6.1 identifies five routines that are associated with model construction. `Construct_the_model` has been discussed previously. The routine called `prime` primes the model from a file. It calls the subsidiary routine `insert_char`, also described earlier, and `show_progress`, which prints a message indicating the progress of the priming operation. `Insert_char` itself calls `create_node`, which allocates space for a new node and returns a pointer to it. `Prime` and `insert_char` are also used for updating the model.

Making predictions

Figure 6.7 shows pseudocode for the process of actually making predictions. There are three phases. The first (lines 759–762 of `make_a_prediction`) sets up pointers into the long-term memory tree, the second (`find_first_chars`) finds the first characters of all predictions, and the third (`extend_pred`) extends the most probable prediction given its initial character. Figure 6.8 illustrates the process for the example tree constructed previously.

```
745-769.   make_a_prediction(command,              Return pointer to the current prediction
                   prediction, number)
752-755.     create and save a copy of the current context in prev_context[]
   756.     if there was a change of context
   759.       for level = 1 to k                    Clear temporary tree pointers
   759.         curr_pointer[level] = NULL
   760.       for each context character
   ---          print character_number
   761.         for level = k downto 1              Initialize temporary tree pointers
   ---            if level == k then
   ---              print context, character, ":", level
   ---            else print context, " :", level
   762.           curr_pointer[level] =
   762.               find_char(curr_pointer[level-1], character)
   765.       find_first_chars(curr_pointer)        At last! — make the prediction
   768.     extend_pred(curr_pointer, prediction, number)


774-800.   find_first_chars(tree_pointer)      Find first chars of all predictions in context

783-784.     clear the record of predictions already encountered
   785.     for level = k-1 downto 0    Make predictions and add unique ones to first[] list
786-789.       scan from tree_pointer[level]->down for each character
   790.         if character is not in the record of predictions then
   791.           add it to the record
   792.           add it to the first[] list
   798.     for each character in zero_freq[] table    Fill out list to include all chars
   799.       if character is not in the record of predictions then
   800.         add it to the first[] list


805-826.   extend_pred(tree_pointer)           Extend a prediction, given its initial character

   816.     the_character = first[pred_number]         Start with the first prediction
   817.     copy tree_pointer[] into t[]
   818.     until desired prediction length is reached
819-820.       add the_character to prediction buffer
   821.       for level = k downto 1                Adjust t[] tree ptrs to the new context
   822.         t[level] = find_char(t[level-1], the_character)
   823.       the_character = best_pred(t)                Extend the prediction


831-846.   find_char(current_level_pointer,            Scan the model for predictions
                   the_character)
   837.     if current_level_pointer is NULL then current_pointer = NULL
   838.     else
   839.       current_pointer = current_level_pointer->down
   840.       for ever                       Check the current level's "down" pointer
   841.         if current_pointer is NULL then goto exit
   842.         if current_pointer->the_character = the_character then
   ---            print found
   842.           goto exit
   ---          print current_pointer->the_character, ", "
   843.         current_pointer = current_pointer->next
         exit:
   ---      print newline
844-846.     return(current_pointer)


851-862.   char best_pred(tree_pointer)    Return best prediction for the current context

854-855.     level = k-1                              Current level in tree
   856.     for ever
   857.       the_prediction = tree_pointer[level]->down->the_character
858-859.       if the_prediction is not NULL return(the_prediction)
   860.       else level = level-1
```

The aim of the first phase is to create pointers into the model, based on the current context, for each context length from 4 through to 1. For example, the bottom part of Figure 6.8a shows a pointer for each of the contexts T#T, #T, and T. These pointers are created by the loop in lines 759–762 of Figure 6.7, and Figure 6.8a shows the state of the pointers after each character of context has been processed (by the outer loop). The inner loop updates each element of the array `curr_pointer[]` for the current context. The `find_char` routine that it calls is identical with `insert_char`, discussed previously, except that it does not update the tree. `Find_char` returns a pointer to the current context, except when passed a null pointer in which case it returns null.

It may not be immediately clear why it is necessary to reconstruct `curr_pointer[]` before each prediction. In fact, the code for constructing the model that was discussed in the preceding subsection will have left the array `last_pointer[]` pointing to the correct context in the tree. However, it is necessary to allow for the possibility that the context changes completely due to the user editing the previous characters. Consequently the pointers are always reconstructed from the current context immediately before making a prediction. The array `curr_pointer[]` is used instead of `last_pointer[]` in order to preserve the latter in the state it was in when the tree was last updated – this is necessary because tree updates are delayed until the end-of-line character is received.

The second phase (`find_first_chars`) finds the first characters of all predictions and adds them to the array `first[]`. Using the `curr_pointers`, it scans through each level of the tree and picks out the characters predicted at that level. Care is taken to ensure that each character in the list only occurs once by ignoring predictions at lower orders that duplicate ones already encountered. This is done using an array `pred_set[]`, which keeps track of the characters predicted so far: The appropriate bit is set as each one is predicted. Once the tree has been scanned, the zero-frequency table is used to fill out the list to include all members of the character set. Figure 6.8b shows the `first[]` array at the end of this phase using the same tree and contexts as Figure 6.8a. No characters are predicted at levels 4 and 3, and a total of seven are predicted at levels 2 and 1. The remainder come from the zero-frequency table shown in Figure 6.3a.

The third phase (`extend_pred`) extends predictions. Although the first character of each prediction has been generated, only the most probable is extended at this point. If the user asks for alternative predictions, `extend_pred` will be called again with a different initial character. Menu versions of the Reactive Keyboard adopt a different strategy, as discussed in Chapter 5.

Figure 6.7. Pseudocode for making predictions.

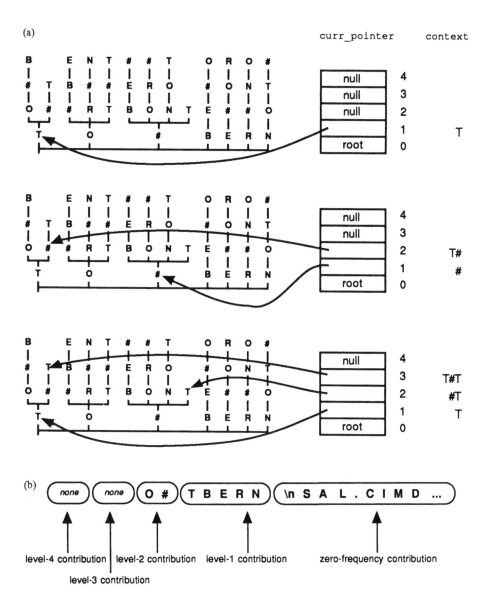

Figure 6.8. Making a prediction: (a) initializing pointers, (b) initial-letter predictions, and (c) extending the best prediction.

Figure 6.8c illustrates the process of extending predictions. The first character of the prediction is "O" – the most likely, according to Figure 6.8b. It is extended first by adding #, then B, then E, to create the concatenated prediction O#BE – which, in fact, is what Shakespeare originally wrote! In practice, it would be extended further until end of line was predicted or either the width of the display or max_ len was reached. The full prediction would be something like

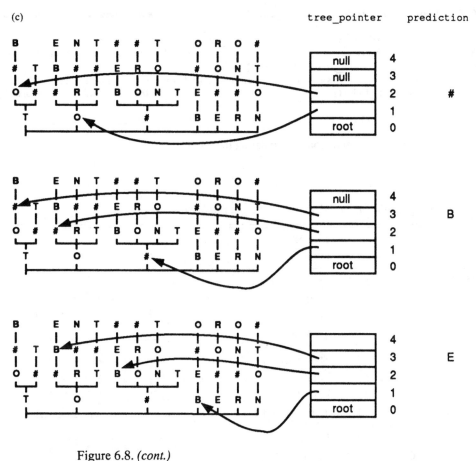

Figure 6.8. *(cont.)*

O#BE#OR#NOT#TO#BE#OR#NOT#TO#BE#OR#NOT#TO#BE,

somewhat less dramatic than Hamlet's actual soliloquy.

The process of extending predictions has been discussed in Chapter 3. The context is shifted and used to form a new prediction until the desired length is reached. Find_char sets pointers into the tree, and best_pred returns the best prediction based on those pointers.

Updating the model

After each prediction is accepted, the model must be updated. The update is delayed until the current command line is completed so that any errors that are corrected by editing the line are not incorporated into the model. As Table 6.1 shows, the update_the_model routine is called by execute_a_command. In fact, update_the_model is identical to make_a_prediction with the

```
867-886.   update_the_model(command_line)        Incorporate a command line into the model

    873.        for each character in command_line
    874.            for level = k downto 1           Insert each character into the model
    875.                last_pointer[level] =
    876.                    insert_char(last_pointer[level-1], character)
877-878.        log_to_file()                        Save the command for future priming

879-886.        update the last_chars[] buffer from tail of command_line
```

Figure 6.9. Pseudocode for updating the model.

Table 6.3. *Updating the model after accepting a prediction*

	Context	Level	insert_char reports	Total nodes	Long-term memory
15	T#T	O : 4	Start added O	44	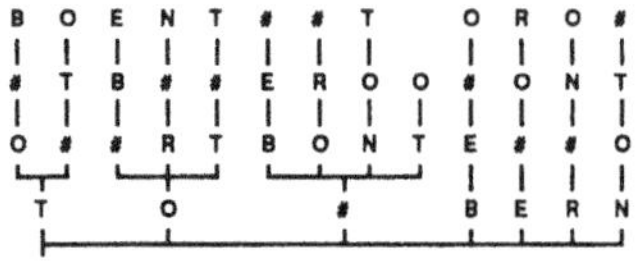
	#T	: 3	Start added O	45	
	T	: 2	Found		
		: 1	T, Found		
16	#TO	# : 4	Start added #	46	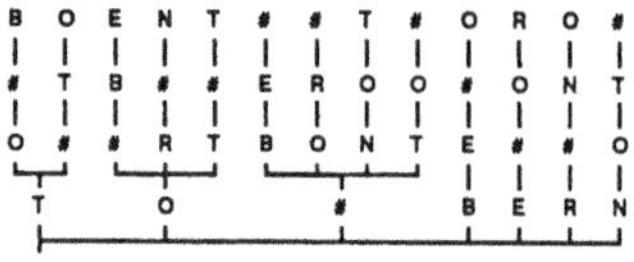
	TO	: 3	Found		
	O	: 2	Found		
		: 1	T,O, Found		
17	TO#	B : 4	Found		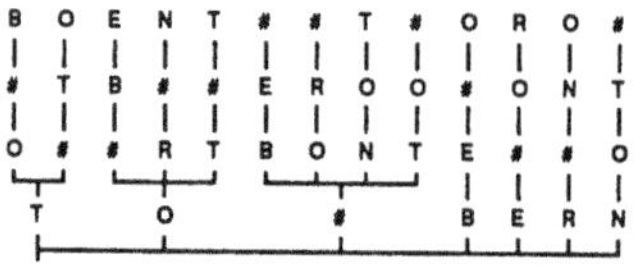
	O#	: 3	Found		
	#	: 2	Found		
		: 1	T,O,#, Found		
18	O#B	E : 4	Found		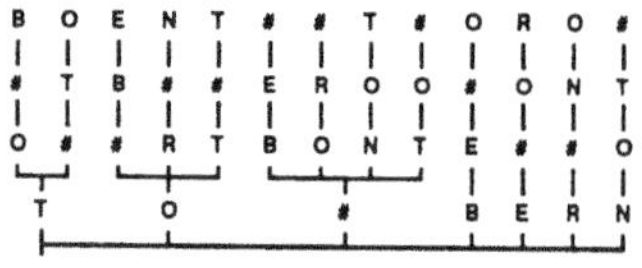
	#B	: 3	Found		
	B	: 2	Found		
		: 1	T,O,#,B, Found		

exception that it uses insert_char to update the model rather than find_char to merely locate predictions.

Figure 6.9 shows the update code, and its effect is illustrated in Table 6.3. When the routine update_the_model is entered, the last_pointer[] array already indicates the correct places in the tree for the first character of the command – this is why make_a_prediction and extend_prediction took care to use curr_ `pointer[ ]`, a copy of `last_pointer[ ]`, rather than `last_pointer[ ]` itself. Each character of the completed command line is inserted at each level of the tree. This is the same as the loop already discussed under model construction (Figure 6.5).

The first part of Table 6.3 shows the insertion of the accepted character, "O," by the `insert_char` routine into two places of the tree, levels 4 and 3. These entries will receive an initial count of 1. Counters corresponding to the relevant occurrences of "O" at levels 2 and 1 will be incremented by the `insert_char` routine. The second part shows "#" being inserted in one place at level 4; its count will be incremented at levels 3, 2, and 1. The following two accepted characters "B" and "E" are found at all levels of the tree and do not cause any structural changes, although the relevant counters will be incremented.

Whenever counters are incremented in `insert_char`, there is the possibility that they may overflow. The maximum allowable frequency can be set by the user, and is stored in `max_freq`. If it is exceeded then all the frequency counts at that level of the tree for that context are halved by the loop in lines 675-679 of Figure 6.5.

Once the tree has been updated, the command line is written to the log file for use when priming in the future. Finally the context array is set to the end of the command line in preparation for the next prediction, because `make_a_prediction` assumes that k characters of context are always available.

6.4. Alternative data structures

A variety of model storage methods have been considered and some implemented. The method of choice depends largely on the amount of empty storage space and processing power available. Table 6.4 lists some alternative implementations of the model that are described in the following sections. Two fixed length-k models are mentioned briefly because of their speed and ease of implementation and to illustrate input mapping for storage economy. Two tree memory structures are then introduced, which are more complex but provide better predictions.

Simple and mapped tables

The simplest way to store a model is as an array whose dimension is the order of the model (first row of Table 6.4). The single-character frequencies of an order-1 ($k = 1$) model can be stored in a one-dimensional array of length 128 (for the 7-bit ASCII alphabet). The character-pair frequencies of an order-2 model need a two-dimensional array (128 × 128), while an order-3 model requires a three-dimensional array (128 × 128 × 128).

To achieve good predictions it is desirable to use as high an order as possible. An order-3 model requires storage for $128^3 = 2^{21}$ counts, one for every possible triplet of characters. If 6- to 8-bit counts are used the space requirement is 1.5 to 2 Mbyte, which may be excessive. It is therefore worth investigating models intermediate

Table 6.4. *Four storage options*

Option	Advantages	Disadvantages
Tables		
Simple tables	Fast, simple	Wastes space, low order
Mapped tables	Fast, more compact	Static maps, incomplete
Pointers		
Pointer/array	Fast, sortable	Full pointers waste space
Compact array	Fast, more compact	Extra address arithmetic

between the order-2 and order-3 ones (second row of Table 6.4). An order-3 model constitutes, in effect, 128 order-2 models – one for each character that can precede the single-character order-2 context. Intermediate models can be constructed by using less than 128 order-2 models – say p of them – and mapping the character preceding the order-2 context into p buckets to select the appropriate model. The storage required for each order-2 model is $2^{14} = 16 \times 2^{10}$ counts, and if p buckets are used, the storage needed is $16p \times 2^{10}$ counts. With counts occupying one byte each, $p = 3$ will fit comfortably into a 64 Kbyte address space. This scheme can be further extended by mapping the characters forming the order-1 context into buckets, as well as its predecessor. If there are q such buckets, the storage occupied is $128pq$ counts.

Characters are best assigned to buckets on a frequency basis, in a way that utilizes each bucket approximately equally. A dynamic assignment based upon the actual statistics of the user's text would be ideal. Unfortunately it would cancel any reduction in storage requirements because individual frequency counts would be needed in order to change the disposition of characters into buckets dynamically. For this reason, the assignments must be made statically, on the basis of the character frequencies in a collection of representative text samples.

Significantly better predictions can be generated by mapping characters into buckets in ways that accurately reflect the actual statistics of the text being generated.

With a little extra summation, simple and mapped tables can be used to implement a variable-length model. For example, an order-1 model merely consists of the row totals of an order-2 model. More specifically, suppose there are s symbols, and let i and j be variables that range between 1 and s. Then for each i,

$$\text{order-1}[i] = \sum_{j=1}^{s} \text{order-2}[i][j]$$

These summations can be avoided by extending the range of j to $1 \ldots s + 1$ and adding an extra column to hold the order-1 model. Then each time order-2$[i][j]$ is

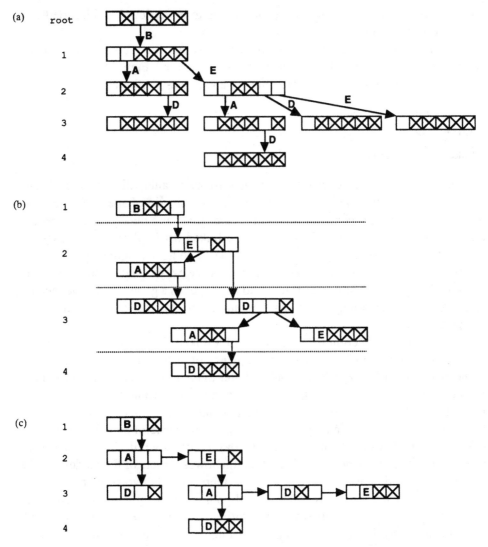

Figure 6.10. Three tree data structures: (a) n-way tree, (b) binary tree, and (c) linked list.

incremented, the order-1 model stored in the extra column order-2$[i][s + 1]$ should be incremented as well.

Variable-length trees

The variable-length tree model described in Chapter 5 can be implemented in many different ways. The usual method of representing trees is to include with each node two or more pointers to its children. Although other linear representations are possible, they do not allow the leaves of the tree to be retrieved and inserted in a time proportional to its depth.

It is important to recognize the distinction between the type of node storage employed (Table 6.4) and the way the nodes are structured. Figure 6.10 gives three examples of how nodes can be represented in a variable-length tree structure:

an n-way tree

a binary tree

a linked-list implementation

Each node of the n-way tree contains a pointer for every alternative at its level. The last two representations are named according to how the list of alternatives at each level is stored. In the second, the alternatives are stored as a binary tree, whereas in the third they are stored as a linked list. The linked-list implementation uses the node definition presented in Figure 6.4c. The last two node storage types in Table 6.4 (rows 3–4) can be structured in any of these ways, giving eight possible variants. However, the best tree structure to use depends a great deal on the method employed for node storage. The space requirements for the three structures are compared below.

As mentioned in Section 6.2, each node of a linked-list tree representation has four parts: a character element label, a frequency of occurrence counter, a pointer to the next alternative at its level, and a pointer to the next level's list of continuations (see Figures 6.4b and 6.10c). A binary tree version would have both left and right alternative pointers, for a total of three pointers per node (Figure 6.10b). An n-way tree would be extremely space intensive and wasteful as most of the 128 pointers per node would be null (Figure 6.10a). Frequency ordering and the small number of descendents per node – at all but the lowest orders of the model – make the linked list option most attractive, because there are only two pointers per node.

If memory space is at a premium, stored pointer size can be minimized at the cost of some extra address arithmetic by storing nodes in a *compact array* (fourth row of Table 6.4). Instead of storing full pointers, compact arrays store an index whose size is

$$\left\lceil \log_2 \frac{\text{number of nodes}}{\text{size of node}} \right\rceil \text{bits.}$$

Pointers are easily recreated by multiplying the stored index by the node size and adding this value to the address of the start of the array. Additional space savings accrue if memory size is substantially smaller than that which can be addressed by pointers. For example, for nodes using 7-bit labels and 7-bit counts, two 17-bit compact array indexes fit comfortably into 6-byte nodes (7 + 7 + 17 + 17 bits). An equivalent 32-bit pointer representation would require 10 bytes per node (7 + 7 + 32 + 32 bits). The compact array example could store 128×2^{10} nodes in 768

Table 6.5. *Space requirements for three tree data structures*

Tree	Bits per mode	Memory access	
		Per level for key retrieval	Per node for a traversal
n-way	$np + d$	1	n
Binary	$3p + d + \lceil \log_2 n \rceil$	$\log_2 c$	3
Linked list	$2p + d + \lceil \log_2 n \rceil$	$\frac{1}{2}c$	2

Note: p = bits in a pointer; d = bits in a data field; n = maximum children per tree node; c = actual number of children for a tree node.

Kbytes, whereas using standard pointers, only 76.8×2^{10} nodes could be stored in the same space. Using the compact representation, 1.7 times as many nodes can be stored.

Storage comparison

Tree structures can be very expensive in terms of storage space, even for low-order models. The method of choice depends on the application context, the total storage space available, and the speed of the computer system. This section looks at the three different tree representations that are sketched in Figure 6.10. Table 6.5 summarizes the results derived below.

The first representation uses an n-way tree. Each node contains n pointers together with the data associated with the node. This gives a total of $np + d$ bits per node where p is the number of bits per pointer and d is the number of bits for the data (Table 6.5). To retrieve on a single key takes one pointer dereference per level in the tree. A tree traversal requires n pointer dereferences per node in the tree (including interior nodes). If n is large this representation is very wasteful of space – entirely in the form of null pointers.

The second tree representation uses three pointers per node. Two are used to construct a binary tree of the children of a given tree node. The third pointer indicates the next level of the tree. In addition each node needs a label of $\lceil \log_2 n \rceil$ bits (the character, in Figure 6.10b) to indicate which child within a particular level it is. This gives a total of $3p + d + \lceil \log_2 n \rceil$ bits per node. If there are c children for a particular node, on the order of $\log_2 c$ memory accesses are needed per level to retrieve a key. Three memory accesses are needed per node when traversing the tree.

The third and final representation uses a linked list at each level instead of a binary tree, giving $2p + d + \lceil \log_2 n \rceil$ bits per node for the pointer form. The search time is increased to $\frac{1}{2}c$ accesses per level. For a traversal, two accesses are needed per node.

6.5. Summary and further reading

The Reactive Keyboard's prediction mechanism is embodied in the three main prediction routines discussed in this chapter: `construct_the_model`, `make_a_prediction`, and `update_the_model`. These routines form the core of the other versions of the system, although their user interfaces are quite different. Other interfaces to the same predictive mechanism could easily be built.

There are various options for implementing the adaptive model that forms the core of the system. The actual implementation uses a simple form of tree-structured memory. This is quite adequate for real-time interaction – the IBM PC system responds instantaneously after each keystroke. Moreover, it is fairly economical with storage, and relatively few nodes are required to model ordinary command-line interactions. By default the system is initialized with 8,000 nodes of storage, which consume 50 Kbyte, and this seems adequate for normal interaction.

There is a further alternative for storing tree structures in a very compact manner, using a data storage technique called "compact hashing" introduced by Cleary (1984) and Cleary and Darragh (1984). It is described in the context of the Reactive Keyboard by Darragh (1988) and Darragh et al. (1991).

Arnott and Javed (1990) describe a character disambiguation scheme for reduced keyboards based on variable-length contexts that is a good application for the mapped tables described in Section 6.4.

7
Concluding remarks

Although good touch-typists are likely to find the Reactive Keyboard a hindrance – except for occasional text generation in a keyboardless graphics interface – moderate to poor typists may find it worthwhile for highly structured text, whereas people with no keyboard experience, or those who cannot use standard keyboards efficiently such as high-level quadriplegics, may view it as an indispensable writing aid. Of all potential users, those with severe physical limitations and communication disabilities stand to gain the most. Although RK-Pointer is new and there is not yet much field experience to go on, RK-Button has been operational for some time, and many people have found it a valuable time- and energy-saving device when writing or accessing computer systems.

The Reactive Keyboard improves on earlier systems in three important ways. First, it uses adaptive modeling, basing its predictions on previously entered text instead of a standard dictionary, and provides convenient facilities for priming with samples of text appropriate to the task at hand. Second, it concatenates predictions, each line in the menu being constructed character by predicted character. RK-MAC also takes advantage of two-dimensional selection to give users the opportunity to maximize the productivity of each selection. Third, its variable-length modeling technique offers higher-quality predictions – as has been shown (indirectly) in numerous text compression experiments. By combining these three improvements within a smooth user interface, it represents a worthwhile advance over earlier predictive text generation systems.

The beneficial effects of adaptation are very striking, and although it is not possible to convey this in brief written examples, user comments serve to indicate how helpful it can be. For instance, one long-standing user has a progressive neuromuscular disorder; he moves extremely slowly and is otherwise unable to write. He employs the system as a general command interface and writing aid, and remarks:

I find the Reactive Keyboard to be an extremely beneficial tool for typing. Since I have severe neurological damage in my hands, it seems to cut the time I spend coding manyfold. To illustrate this, I need only inform you how I mailed John this letter. All that was required was my typing ma, after which time it predicted il·darragh^J. So, I was able to type and enter a command normally requiring thirteen keystrokes in but three! This saves much time since it is rather difficult for me to access some keys on the board. It must be remembered that both my hands and fingers move slowly and inaccurately.

The attention given to both the predictive modeling technique and user interface issues results in a synergy that is unprecedented in communication aid design. The

Reactive Keyboard has great potential to enhance the ease and rate of communication, especially for certain physically limited people.

Full manuals for the UNIX and IBM PC versions of the Reactive Keyboard are reproduced in Appendixes A and B respectively. Both of these systems have interactive online help facilities. The Macintosh version does not have a printed manual, for it is simple to use and the comprehensive online documentation suffices to answer any queries.

All versions of the Reactive Keyboard are free. There is no shareware fee. Users are encouraged to make and distribute as many copies as they wish. Up-to-date versions are available electronically via "anonymous ftp" (file transfer protocol) from `fsa.cpsc.UCalgary.CA` (Internet 136.159.2.1), or by writing to the authors at the University of Calgary (email `darragh@cpsc.UCalgary.CA`).

These systems are provided in source form so that they can be modified to suit different people's requirements. If you do modify them, please tell us so that others will be able to benefit from your efforts.

Appendix A

Documentation for RK-UNIX

The UNIX version of RK-Button is the most comprehensive implementation of the Reactive Keyboard. As well as RK itself, there are three other programs:

> SETUP   for changing RK global variables
>
> RKFREQ   for building a character frequency distribution table
>
> KBDCHECK   to display the characters generated by your terminal

A.1. The RK program

```
rk [- options]
```

The Reactive Keyboard (RK) is a general-purpose command-line editor with the addition of predictive text generation. It interfaces with a standard shell and allows simple editing of input lines. It will also predict new characters based on previous input.

It has several online help facilities, described under "Help" below. For a list of command-line options, invoke with the —h option.

If you just want to get going, skip to the section labeled "Brief Introduction."

Predictive text generation

The Reactive Keyboard accelerates typewritten communication with a computer system by predicting what the user is going to type next. To enable it to make predictions, a model of previously entered text is created and maintained adaptively. (The modeling technique was developed for use in text compression, and forms the basis of one of the most effective compression methods known.) This generally contains a large number of recurring selection element sequences (n-grams), with associated occurrence frequencies. The current context, recent selections, is used to look up likely continuations.

The basic idea is to order context-conditioned candidate strings, which are predicted by the model, according to popularity and display them for selection. Each prediction starts with a different ASCII character, so that the entire character set can always be accessed. Displayed options are actually concatenations of several predicted characters. With the standard keyboard interface the user can cycle through these predictions and accept all or part of any one. Accepted predictions appear to the computer system as though the user had typed them by hand.

Obviously predictions are not always correct, but they are correct often enough to form the basis of a useful communication device. Because they are created adaptively, based on what the user has already typed in this session or in previous ones, the system conforms to whatever kind of text is being entered. Prediction accuracy improves continually as user history accumulates.

Present implementations have proved most useful in enhancing the command interface to the UNIX operating system by predicting commands, arguments, and filenames; and for the entry of free text. Although designed as a general purpose computer interface, RK also has great potential to enhance the ease and rate of communication for physically limited people.

Technical description

RK opens a shell (as defined by your SHELL environment variable) on a pseudo-terminal ("pty"). Any input typed by the user is sent to the standard input of the shell. Any output from the shell is simply sent to the screen. The advantage of this arrangement is that programs do not need to do anything special to work with RK.

It automatically switches off when a program – for example, a screen editor – is competing for control of the input stream. Other programs can be run with RK turned off using the `run_tty_program` function.

RK sets the environment variable RK in the newly created shell. This allows other programs to detect its presence.

Brief introduction

When you first run RK, you'll see a welcome and version message, and then the message

```
Please wait until your shell prompt appears
("^[?" for help)
```

will appear. After a pause, you will see your normal shell prompt,

```
$ ^J
```

with the cursor sitting on the carat (^) sign. Your terminal is *not* broken! The underlined text indicates RK's prediction, which is normally displayed on your screen in inverse video. New text is inserted at the current position of the cursor. The ^J is a newline, that is, a "return" character. Because RK doesn't have any data about your predictions, it's guessing an empty line.

There are several options to control how much of this prediction appears and when. You can accept part or all of it. If you don't want to see predictions, press ^[P (Escape followed by capital letter P; throughout this manual the escape key is denoted by ^[). You can always turn them on again by pressing ^[P again.

RK is also a complete line editor. It allows motion, (automatic) insertion, deletion, and even a crude cut-and-paste buffer. The most recent lines you have entered are placed in a circular pool of buffers, which are recallable. Each line has its own cut buffer.

Filenames and commands can be completed upon request. A filename or command matching the current word, either as a prefix (as in morning*) or a glob expression (as in *.c), is expanded automatically. Unfortunately, RK sometimes loses track of your current working directory. The new_working_directory command can be used to fix this when necessary.

Predictions get better and better as time goes on. Enjoy.

Options

The following options are given in the same order as would be listed by rk −h: first the options with filename arguments, then those with numeric arguments, and finally ones that toggle the values of Boolean variables. We have adopted the convention that options that are only available as command-line arguments are written in lower case. Some options that toggle the values of Boolean variables are also available interactively while RK is running, and are given as the corresponding uppercase character. Their default key bindings are Escape-<command flag>.

Many of RK's command options can be set up in advance using the SETUP utility program, in which case RK should be invoked with the −d option to ensure that this setup information is read. If −d is not given, the internal defaults and command arguments are used.

Filename arguments

−k <key bindings file>

> The file to read new key bindings from (default: $HOME/.rk.keys). This feature allows RK to emulate any number of popular text editors. The built-in key bindings are like *vi*(1). The .rk.keys file supplied with RK sets bindings to be similar to Unipress EMACS. Bindings can be easily modified; see "Changing key bindings" below. Key bindings can also be read interactively using the input_key_bindings command.

−p <prime file>

> The file used to prime the predictive model (default: $HOME/.rk.log_file). Unless −q is also specified, this file will also be used to log any commands or text that you type.

−q <(quaint) log file>

> The file to log all text or commands that RK generates (default: $HOME/.rk.log_file, or the file specified with the −p option). Normally the log file is the same as the priming file; −q allows it to be different. For example, specify −q /dev/null if you want to avoid logging this session. This is a

rarely used feature and is really only deemed "quaint" to make it start with an unused letter.

−z <zero-frequency file>

(default: $HOME/.rk.zero_freq if present, or otherwise the built-in zero-frequency table). See under "Zero-frequency file" below.

Numeric arguments

−b <buffers to save>

The number of buffers available to RK to save previous commands used by previous_line and next_line (default: 77). Because one buffer is always cleared after entering a line of input, you need to allocate one more buffer than the number of lines you wish to recall. For instance, if you want to recall 10 commands, allocate 11 buffers.

−e <end-of-line length>

The maximum length of predictions at the end of the line (default: 42 characters). When using RK over a slower terminal line, it is useful to shorten the prediction length.

−f <frequency count maximum>

The maximum frequency count for any given context (default: 127; range 3 to 255). This count affects the predictive model's specificity in certain contexts, but does not affect the overall speed or space complexity of the predictive algorithm.

−i <in-line length>

The maximum length of predictions in the middle of the line (default: 8). This number is only used when either the −O or −E option is set.

−m <memory maximum>

This argument controls the maximum amount of memory the predictive model will use, in Kbyte (default: 4,096 Kbyte). After this threshold is passed, RK will continue to make predictions, but will cease to learn from your input.

−n <number of prime characters>

The maximum number of characters (*note:* not Kchars) to be read from the prime file at start-up (default: 32,000).

In order to speed start-up on a loaded system, whenever the 15-minute system *uptime*(1) average exceeds one, RK divides the number of prime characters by the uptime average to arrive at a smaller number to read from the prime file. If the prime file is to be truncated it is always the first part that is omitted, to ensure that RK's predictions are based on your most recent work.

−o <order of model>

This argument controls how deep a tree will be built by RK in order to make predictions (default: 8; minimum: 3). As it increases, the accuracy of predictions increases, but the speed decreases. The model order is essentially a count of the number of previous characters you have typed that will be fed into the predictor.

The worst-case space and time complexities of the predictive algorithm increase as this parameter increases. If you get adventurous with high values for −o, be sure to use the show_free_nodes command to see the effect of your choice. Experience has shown that every increment approximately doubles the number of nodes used by the model.

Lowercase toggles

−c   Cut prime file. RK's log file will normally grow without bound. −c remedies this by cutting the prime file during initialization to the default maximum priming size or the value of the −n option. The tail of the file is kept so that the most recent events are saved. The old prime file is saved in <filename>.old. This assumes that the log file and prime file are the same file (which is usually the case, but −q can be used to specify a separate log file).

−d   Default values. Used to read a "setup" file ($HOME/.rk.defaults) at the beginning of a session. The defaults file is an alternative to using command arguments. It is created using the separate SETUP utility program. If −d is not given, internal defaults and command arguments are used. Any options given after −d on the command line supersede those in .rk.defaults.

−l   Login shell. RK normally does not open a login shell. This means the user's .login will be not be run and it is possible to quit RK by typing exit. This option causes RK to open a login shell (in particular, *csh* will run .login). In this case you may exit RK by typing logout. See "Running RK" below.

−h   Help. This causes a short summary of the command-line arguments to be printed, after which RK exits.

−s   Silent start-up. Skips the normal start-up messages.

−u   Underline. Predictions are displayed in underline instead of standout mode. This is useful with certain termcaps, such as SUN.

−v   Version. Prints the version number of RK and exits.

−8   8-bit mode. Normally, RK strips the parity bit off keyboard input. Certain keyboards allow a "meta" character to be generated with the high bit set. This option retains the high bit. See "Changing key bindings" below.

Uppercase toggles

−A (toggle_add_space_mode)
> When you use word movement (accept_forward_word, back-space_word, and so forth), the default is to move to the beginning of a word − that is, so that subsequent text insertion will tend to prepend to words.

With −A specified, the default is to move to the end of a word, so that subsequent text insertion will tend to append to words.

−E (`toggle_eol_longer_mode`)
By default, predictions made at the end of a line are longer than those made in the middle of a line. The −E option disables this feature, in which case the prediction lengths are those given by −i. If predictions at the end of a line are permitted to be longer (the default), the length of the given prediction will be shortened to fit on the current display line.

−I (`toggle_include_stuff_mode`)
Like −A above, but skips over leading spaces, and so on, during word movement.

−L (`toggle_lisp_mode`)
Turns on LISP mode, which automatically matches parentheses.

−N (`toggle_nl_truncate_mode`)
Normally, predictions stop at the end of a line. −N causes RK to continue making predictions past the end of the line, allowing several commands to be predicted at once. However, commands are executed as soon as end-of-line (^J) is accepted.

−O (`toggle_only_at_eol_mode`)
RK normally never displays predictions in the middle of a line. With −O, predictions will be displayed no matter where the cursor is.

−P (`toggle_prediction_mode`)
Disables display of predictions. RK still reads all input, and predictions are still made, but they are not displayed.

−R (`toggle_record_all_mode`)
When writing text to its log file, RK normally does not write blank lines. With −R, these are also written.

−S (`toggle_show_eol_mode`)
When RK predicts a line, it shows the whole line up to and including the return (^J) at the end. With −S, the return is not displayed. To avoid obscuring line breaks, −S has no effect whenever −N is used to predict beyond the end of line.

−W (`toggle_wrap_mode`)
RK normally tries not to wrap lines. −W allows them to be wrapped. This may cause display anomalies on some terminals. Don't lie to UNIX about your terminal, especially about whether or not it has automargins ("am").

Examples

`rk −sP`
Silently open a shell with the line editor enabled but predictions turned off.

```
rk  −h
```
Just print help for the command-line arguments.

```
rk  −o5
```
Run the predictions, but make the order of the model only 5 instead of the default of 8.

```
rk  −z  cfreq  −p  cprimefile
```
Load the file `cfreq` into the zero-frequency table and prime the prediction mechanism with the file `cprimefile`. Using these two arguments, it is possible to set up different environments for prediction. In the above example, `cfreq` could have been created using a large C source file as input and `cprimefile` could be another large C source file. With these inputs, the input of C programs will be simplified, because RK will predict common variable names and keywords.

Running RK

RK may be run manually by typing `rk`. When you want to stop using it, log out in the normal manner. You will be returned to the shell from which you invoked RK.

RK may be run automatically each time you log in. The trick is to start out in a shell that you do not normally use, then automatically reset your shell to the one you do use, set any terminal specific parameters (using *mesg, biff, stty,* and *term,* etc.), and then execute RK as a login shell.

What you do (one time only) is type the following commands, where `login_name` represents the name you type when you log in.

If you normally use *csh*(1), type `chsh login_name`, and put the following *sh*(1) script in a file named `~/.profile`.

```
SHELL=/bin/csh                    # reset to your normal shell
export SHELL
mesg y                            # set mesg and/or biff
stty erase '^H' intr '^?' kill '^['
                                  # set up your terminal
                                  # set any TERMCAP stuff
exec rk −l                        # then exec RK as a login shell
```

If you normally use *sh*(1), type `chsh login_name /bin/csh`, and put the following *csh*(1) script in a file named `$HOME/.login`.

```
setenv SHELL /bin/sh              # reset to your normal shell
mesg y                            #set mesg and/or biff
stty erase '^H' intr '^?' kill '^['
                                  # set up your terminal
                                  # set any TERMCAP stuff
exec rk −l                        # then exec RK as a login shell
```

Tailor this .profile (or .login) to your own needs. The key is to change the shell back to your regular one, set any terminal specific parameters that you want, then exec rk −l. Your normal .login (or .profile) can remain unchanged and is still used when rk −l is executed.

One caution is that you may have to move any commands in your normal .login (or .profile) that change tty access bits into your new .profile (or .login). Otherwise, when RK is invoked as a shell, the system will complain that you are not your terminal's owner. This is harmless, but bothersome.

Having done all this, RK will be automatically run whenever you log in again; and when you log out from within RK, you will also be logged out of the system. If you want the option of running a normal shell at login, replace the last line, exec rk −l, with the following:

```
echo −n "Do you want to run rk [n]?"
read answer; echo ' '
if expr "$answer" == y >>/dev/null; then
        exec rk −l
else
        exec /bin/csh
fi
exit
```

This is for *csh*(1) users who have set up automatic RK logins using the method outlined above. *Sh*(1) users will have to vary the syntax a little.

On slower hosts

Some parameters can be tuned to accommodate a slower host system. Start-up priming is the main bottleneck and most of these actions speed priming by reducing the amount of work to be done. Refer to the specific numeric command arguments for further details.

Reduce the model order, −o
    Each decrement roughly halves the model size and the time it takes to prime it.

Increase the maximum frequency count, −f
    Reduces the number of bit shifts used to prevent overflow.

Decrease the maximum memory, −m
    Reduces initial memory allocation time.

Decrease the number of characters to prime, −n
    Reduces model initialization time. This is also done automatically based on the current system load average and the current value of −n.

Decrease the prediction length, −e
> Reduces prediction generation and display time.

Bindable editing commands

Here are all the bindable commands, along with their built-in default bindings. The built-in key bindings are like *vi*(1). If you use the EMACS-like `.rk.keys` file, your bindings will differ – use ^ [? to print a list of current bindings.

Selection control

`accept_forward_char` (^A)
> Accept the next predicted character.

`accept_forward_word` (^G)
> Accept the next predicted word.

`accept_to_end_of_line` (^E)
> Accept the whole predicted line including any newline (^J) characters.

`accept_to_eol` (^P)
> Accept the predicted line up to, but not including, the first newline (^J) character.

`next_pred` (^T)
> Show the next alternative prediction – that is, one that starts with a different character. This is very handy for cycling through alternative pathnames, email addresses, and so on.

`previous_pred` (^Y)
> Show the previous alternative prediction.

Display control

`clear_display` (^R)
> Clear the screen and redraw the current edit line.

`toggle_add_space_mode` (^[A)
> (Same as −A option.) By default, word movement moves to the beginning of a word, so that subsequent text insertion will tend to prepend to words. If `add_space_mode` is false, word movement positions the cursor at the end of a word, so that text insertion will tend to append to words.

`toggle_eol_longer_mode` (^[E)
> (Same as −E option.) By default, predictions made at the end of a line are longer than those made in the middle of a line. If `eol_longer_mode` is turned off, both revert to the length specified by the −i option.

`toggle_include_stuff_mode(^[I)`

> (Same as —I option.) Like `toggle_add_space_mode` above, but skips over leading spaces, and so on, when doing word movement.

`toggle_lisp_mode(^[L)`

> (Same as —L option.) When LISP mode is turned on, RK will automatically match parentheses.

`toggle_nl_truncate_mode(^[N)`

> (Same as —N option.) Normally, predictions stop at the end of a line. If `nl_truncate_mode` is false, RK continues making predictions past the end of the line, allowing several commands to be predicted at once.

`toggle_only_at_eol_mode(^[O)`

> (Same as —O option.) RK normally does not display predictions in the middle of a line. If `toggle_only_at_eol_mode` is true, predictions will be displayed no matter where the cursor is.

`toggle_pred_mode(^[P)`

> (Same as —P option.) If `pred_mode` is false, display and selection of predictions is disabled. RK still reads all input, and predictions are still made, but they are not displayed.

`toggle_show_eol_mode(^[S)`

> (Same as —S option.) When RK predicts a line, it shows the whole line up to and including the return (`^J`) at the end. If `show_eol_mode` is false, the return is not displayed.

`toggle_wrap_mode(^[W)`

> (Same as —W option.) RK normally tries not to wrap lines. `Toggle_wrap_mode` allows them to be wrapped. This may cause display anomalies on some terminals.

Model control

`prime_from_file(^[g)`

> Prime the predictions from a file. This does not change where new commands are logged, but merely augments RK's current model. This feature is particularly useful for adding not only text files, but also the output of UNIX commands. For example,

```
ls good < day
^[gday
```

will add the good filenames into the model for later use. Another example is `^[gmbox` or `^[g.aliases` to add in email addresses.

show_used_nodes (^[q)
> Show statistics about the predictive model. Valuable when tuning RK to your specific host.

toggle_record_all_mode (^[R)
> (Same as −R option.) When writing text to its log file, RK normally does not write blank lines. In record_all mode, these are also written.

Error control (editing)

backspace_char (^?)
> Backspace (delete) a single character.

backspace_word (^W)
> Backspace (delete) a single word.

backward_char (^H)
> Move backward a single character.

backward_paren (^[()
> Move backward to a matching open parenthesis.

backward_word (^[b)
> Move backward a single word.

beginning_of_line (^[^)
> Move to the beginning of the line.

capitalize_word (^[c)
> Capitalize this word. Just one word is capitalized: No increment factor is applied.

close_paren ())
> Close and show matching parenthesis. This only has a visible effect in lisp_ mode.

dash_to_ul_word (^[_)
> Convert −'s to _'s in this word. Just one word is converted: No increment factor is applied.

delete_char (^X)
> Delete a single character.

delete_char_or_insert_eof (^[^X)
> Delete a single character or, if the cursor is at the end of line, insert the end-of-file character. This provides both the Unipress EMACS delete-character and the shell end-of-file facility. It can be used in place of the separate delete_char and insert_eof_char functions.

delete_region_to_killbuffer (^[k)
> Delete the region between the current cursor and the mark, retaining the deleted text in the kill buffer.

`delete_word` (^[d)
　　Delete a single word.

`discard_current_edit_line` (^U)
　　Delete this line.

`discard_rest_of_line` (^[D)
　　Delete rest of line, retaining the deleted text in the kill buffer.

`end_of_line` (^[$)
　　Move to the end of the line.

`exchange_mark_and_set` (^[s)
　　Move cursor to the mark and set the mark to the previous cursor position.

`finish_editing_line` (^J or ^M)
　　Enter this line.

`forward_char` (^L)
　　Move forward a single character.

`forward_paren` (^[))
　　Move to a matching close parenthesis.

`forward_word` (^[w)
　　Move forward a single word.

`increment_factor` (^[*)
　　Execute the next command $4^{presses}$ times. For example, assume that `increment_factor` is bound to ^U and `forward_char` is bound to ^F. If the user types ^U^U^F the cursor will move forward 4^2 or 16 spaces (or to the end of the line if that comes first).

`insert_eof_char` (^D)
　　Send an EOF character. This usually terminates the current program.

`insert_flush_char` (^O)
　　Send a flush character. This toggles bit-bucketing of program output. *Note:* This function is equivalent to BOGUS in AIX and HP-UX.

`insert_interrupt_char` (^C)
　　Send an interrupt character. This usually kills the current process.

`insert_quit_char` (^\)
　　Send a quit character. This usually kills the current process and causes a core image to be dumped.

`insert_start_char` (^Q)
　　Send a start character. See `insert_stop_char` below.

`insert_stop_char` (^S)

Send a stop character. This usually pauses output from a program. RK will stop sending program output to the screen until `insert_start_char` is sent.

Note: The slave pseudo-tty (the user program) is connected to RK by a buffer of significant size. RK will stop reading output from the slave pseudo-tty, which will probably stop its output, but you should be aware that the program may be somewhat ahead of what you see displayed on your screen.

RK will not respond immediately to the `insert_stop_char` command. Some output from the slave is first flushed to the screen. As a consequence, your terminal should not have auto-XOFF/XON mode set, otherwise characters will be lost.

Sometimes a disconcerting situation arises when an `insert_stop_char` is unknowingly received by your shell: RK continues to operate as normal but output from the shell ceases. This is rectified by invoking the `insert_start_char` function.

`insert_suspend_char (^Z)`

Send a suspend character. This usually stops a process.

Because AIX has no job control, this is equivalent to BOGUS in that environment.

`lowercase_word (^[l)`

Convert this word to lower case. Just one word is converted: No increment factor is applied.

`next_line (^F)`

Show the next line buffer.

`open_paren (()`

Open and show matching parenthesis. This only has a visible effect in `lisp_` mode.

`previous_line (^B)`

Show the previous line buffer.

`quote_char (^V)`

Literally insert the next character.

`set_mark (^[m)`

Set the mark at the current cursor position.

`show_mark (^[')`

Show the position of the current mark.

`twiddle_chars (^[x)`

Exchange the previous two characters.

`ul_to_dash_word` (^[–)

> Convert _'s to –'s in this word. Just one word is converted: No increment factor is applied.

`uppercase_word` (^[u)

> Convert this word to upper case. Just one word is converted: No increment factor is applied.

`yank_from_kill_buffer` (^[p)

> Insert the text stored in the kill buffer.

Help

`show_arguments` (^[C)

> Show the current command-line arguments.

`show_bindings` (^[?)

> Show the current key bindings. The list is piped through *more*(1), or the program named by your PAGER environment variable. Alternatively, bindings can be written to a file for later access. For sanity's sake do not rebind this function.

`show_system_toggles` (^[i)

> Show the current system toggle settings, that is, the state of all bindable toggles set either interactively or at the command line.

`show_termcap_info` (^[h)

> Show the user's termcap settings as read from the TERMCAP file. This is useful for debugging display irregularities.

`show_version` (^[v)

> Show the version number and date of RK.

Other

`BOGUS`, `bogus`, or `null`

> Null routine, which merely beeps the terminal bell. If you want to unbind a key, bind it to this command or to `self_insert`. It is not necessary to explicitly null-bind a key if it is being rebound.

`command_completion` (^[^[)

> Expand a command from a prefix or glob expression, using the PATH environment variable. Commands can be wildcarded; see "Glob syntax" below. After pressing `command_completion` once, pressing the repeater function will display other commands that match the given pattern.

> This function makes assumptions about your current working directory. It is possible for RK to become mistaken about your current working directory (see under `new_working_directory` command below).

`file_completion (^])`

> Expand a pathname from the current prefix or glob expression. The prefix or glob expression occurs after the last directory delimiter ("/"). Filenames can be wildcarded; see "Glob syntax" below. After pressing `file_completion` once, pressing the repeater function will display other files that match the given pattern.
>
> This function also makes assumptions about your current working directory. Again, use the `new_working_directory` command to straighten RK out in case of confusion.

`input_key_bindings (^[j)`

> Read key bindings, either from standard input or a given file. This allows you to change key bindings while running RK. It is particularly useful in combination with `show_bindings` when writing or editing your default `.rk.keys` binding file.

`new_working_directory (^[n)`

> RK consists of two processes: a controlling process that drives the terminal and a slave process that runs the shell. The `file_completion` and `command_completion` commands are relative to the current working directory of the controlling process.
>
> RK tracks the current working directory by spying on the *cd* commands given to the slave process. C shell aliases, Bourne shell functions, *pushd, popd,* and the like, will confuse it. In this event you can use the `new_working_directory` command to reset the current working directory of the controlling process. In practice it is often easier to issue a *cd* command to change to the current directory, aided by the file completion command and RK's predictions. Use an absolute pathname, or a relative path from your home directory.

`repeater (^K)`

> This allows you to scroll through the completions that matched your original pattern. It can only be invoked after a `file_completion` or a `command_completion`.

`run_mesg (^[M)`

> Run the *mesg*(1) command. This toggles `mesg` mode on your controlling terminal, rather than on the pseudo-tty running your shell.

`run_ruptime (^[z)`

> Run the *uptime*(1) command (emulates *csh*'s `^T` command).

`run_talk (^[t)`

> Run the *talk*(1) command.

`run_tty_program (^[r)`

> Run a program with RK turned off. This command provides programs with direct access to the current tty modes rather than going through RK's

pseudoterminal. All other commands starting with `run_` (with the exception of `run_uptime`) are special cases of this command.

`run_write(^[y)`

Run the *write*(1) command.

`self_insert`

Literally insert the current character. If you want to remove special meaning from a character, use `self_insert` to allow the character to be literally sent.

To add a new function to the code of RK, you need to add the function name, address, and description to the `kbdbind.c` file, add the function declaration to `functions.h`, and then recompile.

Glob syntax

`Command_completion` and `file_completion` recognize wildcards applied to the command or filename. In the case of `file_completion`, wildcards may not be applied to directories. Glob syntax is what you are accustomed to using for filename expansion in UNIX shells. However, Bourne shell, C shell, and others have different rules for what may be used in a glob expression. Here is what may be used in RK:

`*`	Matches zero or more occurrences of any character
`?`	Question mark matches any single character
`[abc]`	Matches any single character a, b, or c
`[!abc]`	Matches any single character that is not a, b, or c
`[a-z]`	Matches any lowercase character
`[!a-z]`	Matches any character that is not lowercase a through z
`\`	Removes the special meaning of the following character

In the case of `file_completion`, a directory can optionally precede the filename pattern. In this case, patterns of the form `~/foo` and `~user/foo` are accepted.

Changing key bindings

On start-up, RK looks for the file `$HOME/.rk.keys` or a file specified by the −k option. If it exists, new key bindings are read from it. Bindings consist of a function name, followed by a key to bind to in double quotes ("). Empty lines are ignored. Comments begin with "#," in which case the rest of the line is ignored. Control characters may be embedded in the key sequence using the ^ character, so that ^A is control-A.

Use the ^[? command (show_bindings) to see your current bindings. Use input_key_bindings to try out new ones, either interactively or from a file.

Metacharacters (key characters greater than 127) are represented by a preceding exclamation point (!), so for instance, 129 is represented by !^A. Meta-C would be represented by !C, and metacarat would be represented by !\^. Metacharacters may only be entered if the −8 option is used.

The \ character works the same way as the \ character in termcap entries:

\E	Escape (^[)
\b	backspace (^H)
\f	form feed (^L)
\n	newline (^J)
\r	carriage return (^M)
\t	tab (^I)
\\	a single \
\^	^
\177 or ^?	rubout (delete)
^@ or ^space	null (ASCII 0)

If you omit the quotes, the corresponding entry is read from the TERMCAP file. See the manual entry for *termcap*(5) for a complete list of these capabilities. Some of the more useful values are:

K1	keypad upper left (usually Home)
K3	keypad upper right (usually PgUp)
K4	keypad lower left (usually End)
K5	keypad lower right (usually PgDn)
kl	left arrow
kr	right arrow
kd	down arrow
ku	up arrow
k0–k9	function keys

Shorter entries will replace longer ones. For instance, if you bind ^[A to toggle_lisp_mode and subsequently bind ^[to self_insert, you will overwrite the longer binding. RK is rather dumb about this. For example, if you bind ABC and ADE to different functions, and then rebind A, the ABC and ADE bindings cease to work (although they still show up in show_bindings).

For example, a file like:

```
accept_forward_word  "^N"
show_bindings        "^[?"
insert_start_char    "^S"
insert_stop_char     "^Q"
set_mark             "^@"
toggle_lisp_mode     k1
```

would bind ^N to accept_forward_word, ^[? to show_bindings, function key F1 to toggle_lisp_mode, and ^@ to set_mark. It would also reverse the meanings of ^S and ^Q from their defaults.

As another example, the function of the DELETE and BACKSPACE keys can be switched by

```
backspace_char  "^?"
delete_char     "^H"
```

Many people make this switch in their .login, but RK remains oblivious to this unless you explicitly rebind these keys.

Zero-frequency file

When the current input has never been encountered before, RK consults its zero-frequency table, which gives a standard ordering of all characters by frequency. At start-up, it reads the file $HOME/.rk.zero_freq. If this does not exist, a built-in default zero-frequency table is used.

The program RKFREQ will create zero-frequency files for you. By running rkfreq <input_data >output_file, the frequencies of characters in the file input_data will be used to generate the file output_file. To use the new zero-frequency file, either rename it to $HOME/.rk.zero_freq or use the −z option when invoking RK.

Files

rkfreq

> A program to generate zero-frequency files, used with the −z option or .rk.zero_freq.

.rk.defaults

> Generated by the SETUP program to ease parameter setting, and used when RK is invoked with the −d option.

.rk.log_file

> The default file to use to prime the prediction mechanism and store all of the user's input.

`.rk.keys`
> The (optional) default key bindings file. The EMACS-like `.rk.keys` supplied makes RK operate like Unipress EMACS (see "Changing key bindings" above).

`.rk.zero_freq`
> The actual zero-frequency file (see "Zero-frequency file" above).

`setup`
> The program used to generate a new `.rk.defaults` file (see "Options" above).

Authors

John Darragh;   overall concept, predictive mechanism
Dan Freedman;   input line editor
Mark James;   key bindings, command line
Dejan Mitrovic;   setup program
Jason Penney;   display routines
Doug Taylor;   file completion
Ian Witten;   overall concept, coordination

Distribution

The Reactive Keyboard is free. There is no shareware fee. We encourage you to make and distribute as many copies as you wish, for whomever you wish, as long as it is not for profit. The current versions are available electronically via anonymous ftp from `fsa.cpsc.UCalgary.CA` (Internet 136.159.2.1). Versions are available for UNIX, IBM PC, and Apple Macintosh.

It is provided in source form so that it can be modified to suit different people's requirements. If you do modify it, we'd like to hear about it so that others will be able to benefit from your efforts.

RK is a demonstration program, not a commercial product. We cannot offer services such as telephone support, mailing lists, or upgrade services.

Make and hosts

The UNIX version of RK is known to run (more or less) in the following environments:

Sun SunOS 4.0.3	(Sun-3, Sun-4, and Sun-386i)
DEC Ultrix 2.1	(DECstation only, VAX uncertain)
Sony NEWS-OS 3.2	(1850 only, others shouldn't be a problem)
HP-UX 7.0	(300 series only, 800 series uncertain)
IBM AIX 2.2.1	(IBM RT only, other hosts uncertain)

There are minor hitches making RK on the Sun-3 and the IBM RT. See the Makefile for details.

To compile, examine the Makefile and enable the appropriate options. The default options are for most BSD machines. Typing make will create the program in the current directory. If you wish, make install will subsequently install the binaries and man pages into well-known directories.

If you want to run RK on a different host than those listed previously, you're on your own; but don't despair. Conditional compilation exists for BSD, SYSTEM-V, and even some POSIX-derived systems, so it should be possible for you to get RK running on your system by enabling the appropriate spells at different points in the code. BSD is the default case, but you can find most of the points of variation by searching the sources for "AIX."

See also

csh(1), *mesg*(1), *stty*(1), *talk*(1), *tset*(1), *uptime*(1), *write*(1), *pty*(4), *termio*(4), *termcap*(5)

Darragh, J. J. (1988); Darragh, J. J., Witten, I. H. and James, M. L. (1990); and Darragh, J. J. and Witten, I. H. (1991)

Known bugs

The lists created by file_completion and command_completion are cleared as soon as any other function is invoked.

File_completion and command_completion can become confused about the current working directory (see the new_working_directory command in "Bindable editing commands" for an easy workaround).

If file completion or command completion returns a file name with wildcards (i.e., a *, ?, [, or]), the filename will not be properly escaped with back slashes before it is inserted into the edit buffer.

When walking directories, RK always appends a slash to directory names, even when this is inappropriate.

The AIX and HP-UX versions do not properly track changing window sizes. If you log in remotely ("rlogin") through a window that can change size, strange things will happen if you do in fact change its size. Conversely, the use of odd-sized windows may cause graphic programs to misbehave.

RK has to poll to determine whether your program is driving the keyboard in "raw" or "cooked" mode. This poll can occur too late. If so, RK will place a prediction on the screen after a raw-mode program (e.g., a display editor) has assumed control, or omit a prediction following your first shell prompt after leaving it. The superfluous prediction can be removed, or a missing one displayed, by typing RETURN.

RK's model can use all available memory if the priming file and start-up amount are too large.

Certain programs that require access to the parent terminal can only be handled through `run_tty_program`.

Tabs are not echoed properly in the input line, although they do make their way into the input stream.

It is possible to unbind keys by mistake as described above under "Changing Key Bindings."

Default bindings for shell-significant characters like end-of-file should be set by RK to their bindings in the shell environment before RK was invoked. RK currently ignores these.

`Previous_line` clobbers the old command line and loses the current place in the edit buffer list. Instead, it should copy the previous buffer into the current line buffer, leaving both the old buffer and the current position unchanged.

RK does not understand the semantic significance of the lines you type. If you edit a file all day and then issue an `rm` command, it is quite likely to suggest that you `rm` that file. Be careful. Potentially irreversible commands, such as `rm`, should perhaps be aliased to something safer.

Wish list

The file output from the `show_bindings` command should be compatible with the format of the `.rk.keys` file.

General macro assignments should be allowed, so that a function key or other key sequence can be mapped to some other arbitrary string of characters to be inserted in the edit buffer. This would also allow a pseudo-Dvorak keyboard layout to be defined.

While RK reads lines from the prime file at start-up, it does not place the lines in the command line recall buffer. It should, so that `previous_line` and `next_line` can recall commands across RK sessions.

Bug reports

Please report bugs to `darragh@cpsc.UCalgary.CA`. We are also interested in hearing about your experiences using the Reactive Keyboard.

A.2. The SETUP program

The SETUP program is a utility for changing various default command argument settings for the Reactive Keyboard. It is intended to aid users in setting up RK for future use, avoiding the need to specify command arguments whenever RK is invoked.

New values for RK global variables are saved in the file `$HOME/.rk.de-faults`. However, these new settings are not used unless RK is invoked with the –d option. There is currently no way to tell RK to look elsewhere for this file.

Commands

There are two command sets, depending on which part of the menu you are in. The first is used for file names and integer values, the second for boolean values.

^Q   Quit
        Quit SETUP immediately (prompts to save any changes).
^S   Save
        Explicitly save changes to `$HOME/.rk.defaults`. SETUP confirms where it wrote the file.
^R   Reset
        Redraws the screen and resets parameters to their most recently saved values.
^U   Up
        Moves the cursor up to the previous variable.
^D   Down
        Moves the cursor down to the next variable.
^C   Change
        Changes a variable from 0 to 1 or from 1 to 0 (boolean variables only).
<enter new value>
        Type in a new filename or integer value as appropriate, terminated by Return. You can delete an old filename by pressing the Return key immediately. If no file name is given, or an old one is deleted, the word (null) appears in its place. There are no line editing features – the only way to fix errors is to retype the entry. None of the other commands are available while entering a new value.
<CR>
        Carriage return (^J) completes a new filename entry or integer value.

Start-up screen

See the "Options" section of the RK manual entry to determine what these things are. Most of RK's options are available using SETUP. Exceptions are –k <key binding file>, –c, –A, –I, –R, and –W, which are recent additions to RK, and –d, –h, and –v, which are inappropriate for offline setup.

Files

$HOME/.rk.defaults
        New values for RK global variables are saved in this file.

```
   Filenames arguments (valid values= any UNIX file name <CR>):
          -p <prime file>                    (null)
          -q <(quaint) log file>             (null)
          -z <zero frequency file>           (null)
   Numeric arguments (valid values= integers <CR>):
          -b buffers to save                 77
          -e end of line length              42
          -f frequency count maximum         127
          -i inline length                   8
          -m memory maximum                  4096
          -n number of prime characters      32000
          -o order of model                  8
   Upper & lowercase toggles_ (valid values= 0 or 1) use ^C:
          -E (eol_longer_mode)               1
          -L (lisp_mode)                     0
          -N (nl_truncate_mode)              1
          -O (only_at_eol_mode)              1
          -P (prediction_mode)               1
          -S (show_eol_mode)                 1
          -l Login shell                     0
          -s Silent start-up                 0
          -u Underline                       0
          -8 8-bit mode                      0

   Enter: ^Q(uit), ^S(ave), ^R(eset), ^U(p), ^D(own), or ^C(hange)
```

Bugs

The current state of SETUP leaves much to be desired in terms of completeness, variable names versus command-argument names, and general user interface features.

Some new RK command options are not represented.

SETUP does not follow the convention used by RK for optional "default" files, such as .rk.keys, where the file is automatically used if it resides in $HOME, and an override command argument such as rk -k new.keys is used if it resides elsewhere.

Spaces in filenames or integer values cause problems (real problems!) and new values *must* be terminated by carriage return.

Most commands are inoperative during entry of strings; some cause strange effects.

SETUP is written for a 25-line display. It does not work properly on some terminals because of its reliance on relative rather than absolute cursor addressing.

Wish list

Fix the bugs.

Split the code that reads and writes defaults into a separate file for easier access by SETUP and RK (see RK's `read_defaults_file` function).

Add an `input_defaults` command to RK to read new setup defaults interactively.

A.3. The RKFREQ program

```
rkfreq [-c -h <input filename>]
```

The RKFREQ program builds a character frequency distribution for use with the Reactive Keyboard. It is a filter, reading data from standard input and writing a file on standard output that may be passed to RK. The data is used by RK to predict characters that have not yet occurred in its input stream through priming or user commands.

RKFREQ appends any ASCII characters not seen in its input file to its output stream in ASCII sequence, followed by any unrepresented control codes (including DEL).

Without the −c option, RKFREQ prints 128 ASCII characters, each followed by newline. This is the format that RK expects for its default `.rk.zero_freq` file, or any file specified by −z `<filename>`. The newlines are for readability only – RK ignores them.

Options

−c   Create a source file suitable for inclusion in RK source code as a replacement for the default character distribution table `zero_freq[]`.

−h   Print a brief help message.

`<input filename>`
        The name of a large sample of representative text to be used to build the distribution.

Files

`$HOME/.rk.zero_freq`
        The default zero-frequency file used by RK, if present. If not, a built-in default table is used unless a different filename is specified by `rk −z <filename>`.

A.4. The KBDCHECK program

        kbdcheck [−8]

The KBDCHECK program displays the characters generated by your terminal. It is of most interest to verify special keys, such as `cursor up` or `F1`.

To exit the program, type any single character three (3) times consecutively.

This program is in the public domain. Neither the authors nor the maintainers make any claim to it, and no one else has the right.

Options

−8   Reads all 8 bits of keyboard input, including the most significant bit, which is often used as a parity bit. If −8 is not specified, the most significant bit is stripped.

See also

termcap(5)

Appendix B

Documentation for RK-PC

The UNIX version of RK-Button has been ported to the IBM PC to provide a similar predictive interface to MS-DOS. It has been stripped down to reduce resource consumption, and program and model memory together occupy just 80 Kbyte. It responds to keystrokes instantly, without any perceptible delay. In order to reduce the size of memory required, the Reactive Keyboard (RK) is divided into several smaller programs:

RK	command-line editor with predictive text generation
SETUP	for changing RK global variables
HELP	for formatting and printing the help files
CUT_PRIME	for cutting the priming file to a specified size

These programs can be used separately, but SETUP can be accessed from within the RK program (^S command), and HELP can be called from within RK and SETUP (F1 command).

B.1. The RK program

Command-line editor with predictive text generation
Command-line arguments – none

To invoke the Reactive Keyboard, simply type RK. Global variables are initialized by reading a default file, which contains values specified by the last SETUP call. RK constructs the history model and makes its initial predictions. The user can then interact with the computer using the commands outlined below, most of which are invoked by function keys. RK also supports EMACS-like key bindings for some commands, shown in parentheses.

Selection control

Arrow Right (^F)
  Accept one character from the prediction.

End (^E)
  When the cursor is at the end of the line, and a prediction is displayed, End accepts the entire prediction. If accept_to_eol = 1, it accepts the predic-

tion up to but not including new-line/carriage return (^M). Invoke SETUP to determine the status of `accept_to_eol`.

Insert (^W)
>   Accept a word from the prediction.

Page Down
>   Show the next prediction.

Page Up
>   Show the previous prediction.

Editing commands

Arrow Left (^B)
>   Move the cursor to the left.

Arrow Right (^F)
>   When editing the command line with no prediction displayed, `Arrow Right` moves the cursor to the right.

Arrow Up
>   Show the previous command.

Arrow Down
>   Show the next command.

Backspace
>   Delete the character to the left of the current cursor position.

Delete
>   Delete the character at the current cursor position.

End (^E)
>   When editing the command line with no prediction displayed, End moves the cursor to the end of the command line.

Esc (^K)
>   Kill to the end of the line (including prediction).

Home (^A)
>   Move the cursor to the beginning of the line.

Miscellaneous

F1   Help.
^P   Prime from a file.
^Q   Exit the Reactive Keyboard.
^S   Change RK global variables (call SETUP).

B.2. The SETUP program

Simple screen editor for changing RK global variables

Command-line arguments – none

The Reactive Keyboard uses several global variables to control its behavior. These variables, which are listed below, can be modified to tailor RK to your own needs. They are stored in a default file (`rk.def` under the directory where RK is installed), which SETUP reads and modifies.

SETUP can be run from DOS as a separate program or invoked from RK with the ^S command. If called from RK, any new numeric values given to variables are immediately adopted and used.

Commands

`Arrow Up`
    Move the cursor to the previous variable.

`Arrow Down`
    Move the cursor to the next variable.

`^C` Change value (for on/off variables).

`F1` Help.

`^F1` Context-sensitive help.

`^Q` Exit the program.

`^S` Save values to the default file.

RK global variables

After entering new values for the variables, press the ENTER or RETURN key.

Display control

`accept_to_eol`
    Controls the behavior of prediction acceptance. If set to 1 the prediction will be accepted up to but not including the carriage return (^M) when the END key or ^E is typed. If set to 0 the prediction will be accepted, including the carriage return, causing execution of the command when the aforementioned keys are typed.

`display_prompt`
    The DOS prompt (the name of the current directory) will be displayed on the beginning of each line if this variable is set to 1. Otherwise, it will be hidden.

`max_len`
    The length of predictions (values of 20 to 60 are generally good ones).

`pred_mode`
    Display of predictions can be enabled (if 1) or disabled (0).

Model control

`log_file`
> The file to log commands to. This can be the same as the prime file.

`max_freq`
> The maximum frequency for any given context. This count affects the predictive model's specificity in certain contexts but does not affect the overall speed or space complexity of the predictive algorithm. Minimum 3, recommended value 127.

`max_k`
> This variable controls the depth of the tree built by RK that is used to make predictions. As `max_k` increases, the accuracy of predictions increases, but the speed decreases and the memory needed to store the model increases exponentially. The model order is essentially a count of the number of previous characters you have typed that will be fed into the predictor. The worst case space and time complexities of the predictive algorithm increase as this parameter increases. The minimum value is 4, and the recommended value is 7.

`max_nodes`
> This variable controls the maximum number of nodes that the predictive model will use. Each node occupies either 6 or 10 bytes depending on the memory model under which the program is compiled. After this threshold is passed, RK will continue to make predictions, but will cease to learn from your input. Recommended values are a few thousand nodes (for example, 8,000).

`max_prime`
> The maximum number of characters to be read from the priming file at start-up. If this number is less than the size of the priming file, RK will omit the first part of the priming file. In this way, RK's predictive knowledge is biased by your most recent work. This value must be less than or equal to the value of `max_nodes`.

`prime_file`
> The file used to prime the predictive model.

`zero_freq_file`
> A file that gives all ASCII characters in the order of their expected frequency of appearance in text.

B.3. The HELP program

Program for viewing text files – `help [file name]`

If a file is not given, typing HELP at the DOS prompt defaults to paging through `RK.DOC` (this document). If you are not sure about some details concerning RK or

SETUP you can call the HELP program. It will display help files, which can be read using the Page Up and Page Down keys. You can return to your previous work by pressing the Esc key, which exits HELP. You can call HELP from RK or SETUP by pressing function key F1, which will display the help files RK.HLP or SU.HLP respectively. If you add a file name then you can use HELP to display any text file to a maximum of 50 pages in length.

B.4. The CUT_PRIME program

Utility program that cuts a priming file

Command-line arguments – new file size for priming file

If your priming file is the same as your log file (see "RK global variables" above), it will continue to grow in size with every command you enter. In order to save disk space, it is advisable to call CUT_PRIME from time to time.

If no command-line argument is given, the beginning of the priming file will be truncated so that max_prime characters remain (see "RK global variables"). The tail end of the priming file is saved to preserve the most recent user inputs.

Appendix C
Code for the Reactive Keyboard

```
1      /*****************************************************************************
2      *                                                                           *
3      *  rk_com.c -- Command line editor for the Reactive Keyboard                 *
4      *                                                                           *
5      *  external interfaces:                                                      *
6      *      clear_to_end(x, y)  int x, y;                                         *
7      *      get_cursor(&x, &y)  int * x, * y;                                     *
8      *      set_cursor(x, y)    int x, y;                                         *
9      *                                                                           *
10     *****************************************************************************/
11
12
13     #define VERSION "Version 1.3   University of Calgary    February 1991"
14
15     #include <ctype.h>
16     #include <dir.h>
17     #include <dos.h>
18     #include <stdio.h>
19     #include <stdlib.h>
20
21     /* emacs-like key bindings - see the outer switch below                    */
22
23     #define BELL           7                 /* ring the terminal bell         */
24     #define Ctrl_A         1                 /* cursor home                    */
25     #define Ctrl_B         2                 /* cursor back one character      */
26     #define Ctrl_E         5                 /* cursor to end of command       */
27     #define Ctrl_F         6                 /* cursor forward one character   */
28     #define Ctrl_H         8                 /* backspace                      */
29     #define Ctrl_K         11                /* kill to end of line            */
30     #define Ctrl_M         13                /* carriage return or "enter"     */
31     #define Ctrl_P         16                /* prime from file                */
32     #define Ctrl_Q         17                /* leave rk                       */
33     #define Ctrl_S         19                /* call setup                     */
34     #define Ctrl_W         23                /* cursor forward a word          */
35     #define ESC            27                /* same as Ctrl_K                 */
36
37     /* function key definitions each preceded by 0 byte - see inner switch below */
38
39     #define Arrow_Down     80                /* next command in history        */
40     #define Arrow_Left     75                /* cursor back one character      */
41     #define Arrow_Right    77                /* cursor forward one character   */
42     #define Arrow_Up       72                /* previous command in history    */
43     #define DEL            83                /* delete current character       */
44     #define END            79                /* cursor to end of line          */
45     #define F1             59                /* call help file                 */
46     #define HOME           71                /* cursor to beginning of line    */
47     #define INS            82                /* cursor forward a word          */
48     #define PgDn           81                /* next prediction                */
49     #define PgUp           73                /* previous prediction            */
50
51     /* if the ANSI display driver (ansi.sys) is installed, use it              */
52
53     #ifdef ansi
54         #define invon()   printf("\033[7m")   /* ansi inverse on               */
55         #define invoff()  printf("\033[m")    /* ansi inverse off              */
56         #define Printf    printf
57     #else
```

```
58      #define invon()   textattr(0x70)      /* inverse video on           */
59      #define invoff()  textattr(0x07)      /* inverse video off          */
60      #define Printf    cprintf
61   #endif
62
63   #define MAX_HIST       8                  /* number of com_bufs to save */
64   #define MAX_DIR       50                  /* size of a directory name   */
65   #define MAX_SAVE      64                  /* length of each com_buf to save */
66   #define MAX_SET      128                  /* maximum number of symbols  */
67   #define MAX_BUF      256                  /* maximum size of a text buffer */
68   #define FALSE          0
69   #define TRUE           1
70
71   /* global variables                                                     */
72
73   static int     x_position, y_position;    /* start of current line      */
74
75   static char    com_buf[MAX_BUF],          /* entered part of line       */
76                  * c_end   = com_buf,       /* end of command line        */
77                  * current = com_buf,       /* current posn in command line */
78                  prev_buf[MAX_HIST][MAX_SAVE];/* previous commands         */
79   static int     last_command   = 0,        /* index of last command saved */
80                  t_last_command = 0;        /* temporary version of above */
81
82   static char    pred_buf[MAX_BUF];         /* prediction buffer          */
83   static int     pred_number = 0;           /* index of current prediction */
84
85   static char    prompt  = TRUE;            /* need to display DOS prompt? */
86
87
88   /* AWAIT AND PROCESS INPUT KEYSTROKES                                    */
89
90   main()
91   {
92       extern char   accept_to_eol,         /* exclude nl from accept to eol? */
93                     pred_mode,             /* predicting or not?         */
94                     display_prompt;        /* displaying prompt or not?  */
95              char   c, * ptr,              /* input char and generic pointer */
96                     cwd_buf[MAX_DIR],      /* current working directory  */
97                     update_display = TRUE; /* need to redraw command line? */
98              int    x, y;                  /* screen coordinates         */
99
100      printf("Welcome to the Reactive Keyboard\n%s\n", VERSION);
101      printf("For help press Function key F1, or type \"help\" ");
102
103      read_setup();                         /* initialize the model       */
104      construct_the_model();
105
106      printf("\n\n");
107
108      while (1) {                           /* await user actions         */
109
110          if (prompt) {                     /* display user prompt        */
111              if (display_prompt) printf("\n%s>", getcwd(cwd_buf, MAX_DIR));
112              get_cursor( &x_position, &y_position);
113              prompt = FALSE;
114          }
115
116          if (update_display) {             /* display command and prediction */
117              if (pred_mode) make_a_prediction(com_buf, pred_buf, &pred_number);
118              display_line((current == c_end || com_buf == c_end) && pred_mode);
119          }
120          else update_display = TRUE;
121
```

```
122              switch(c = getch()) {                /* outer switch for control keys  */
123
124              case Ctrl_A:                         /* cursor home                    */
125                  ungetch(HOME);
126              goto INNER_SWITCH;
127
128              case Ctrl_B:                         /* cursor back one character      */
129                  ungetch(Arrow_Left);
130              goto INNER_SWITCH;
131
132              case Ctrl_E:                         /* cursor to end of command       */
133                  ungetch(END);
134              goto INNER_SWITCH;
135
136              case Ctrl_F:                         /* cursor forward one character   */
137                  ungetch(Arrow_Right);
138              goto INNER_SWITCH;
139
139              case Ctrl_H:                         /* backspace                      */
140                  if (current != com_buf) {
141                      for (ptr = --current; ptr < c_end; ptr++) *ptr = *(ptr + 1);
142                      *(--c_end) = '\0';
143                  }
144              break;
145
146              case Ctrl_K:                         /* kill to end of line            */
147              case ESC:
148                  c_end = current;
149                  *c_end = '\0';
150              break;
151
152              case Ctrl_M:                         /* carriage return or "enter"     */
153                  execute_a_command();
154              break;
155
156              case Ctrl_P:                         /* prime from file                */
157                  if (current == com_buf) prime_from_file();
158                  prompt = TRUE;
159              break;
160
161              case Ctrl_Q:                         /* leave rk                       */
162                  display_line(FALSE);
163                  exit(0);
164              break;
165
166              case Ctrl_S:                         /* call setup                     */
167                  system("setup");
168                  read_setup();
169                  prompt = TRUE;
170              break;
171
172              case Ctrl_W:                         /* cursor forward a word          */
173                  ungetch(INS);
174              goto INNER_SWITCH;
175
176              case 0:
177
178                  INNER_SWITCH:
179                  switch(getch()) {                /* inner switch for function keys */
180
181                  case Arrow_Down:                 /* next command in history        */
182                      x = t_last_command + 1;
183                      if (x == MAX_HIST) x = 0;
184                      if (*prev_buf[x]) {
185                          t_last_command = x;
186                          *com_buf = '\0';
```

```
187                         strcpy(com_buf, prev_buf[x]);
188                         c_end = current = com_buf + strlen(com_buf);
189                     }
190                     else putchar(BELL);
191                 break;
192
193                 case Arrow_Left:              /* cursor back one character    */
194                     if (current < c_end) update_display = FALSE;
195                     if (current > com_buf) {
196                         current--;
197                         get_cursor(&x, &y);
198                         set_cursor(--x, y);
199                     }
200                 break;
201
202                 case Arrow_Right:             /* cursor forward one character */
203                     if (current < c_end) {
204                         if (++current != c_end) {
205                             get_cursor(&x, &y);
206                             set_cursor(++x, y);
207                             update_display = FALSE;
208                         }
209                     }
210                     else if (*pred_buf == '\n') execute_a_command();
211                     else if (*pred_buf) {        /* accept first predicted char   */
212                         *current++ = *pred_buf;
213                         c_end = current;
214                         *c_end  = '\0';
215                     }
216                 break;
217
218                 case Arrow_Up:                /* previous command in history   */
219                     if (*prev_buf[t_last_command]) {
220                         *com_buf = '\0';
221                         strcpy(com_buf, prev_buf[t_last_command]);
222                         c_end = current = com_buf + strlen(com_buf);
223                         if (--t_last_command < 0) t_last_command = MAX_HIST - 1;
224                     }
225                     else putchar(BELL);
226                 break;
227
228                 case DEL:                     /* delete current character      */
229                     if (current < c_end) {
230                         for (ptr = current; ptr < c_end; ptr++) *ptr = *(ptr + 1);
231                         c_end--;
232                     }
233                 break;
234
235                 case END:                     /* cursor to end of line         */
236                     if (current < c_end) current = c_end;
237                     else if (*pred_buf == '\n') execute_a_command();
238                     else {                     /* accept entire prediction      */
239                         strcat(com_buf, pred_buf);
240                         c_end += strlen(pred_buf);
241                         current = c_end;
242                         if (*(c_end - 1) == '\n') {
243                             current = --c_end;
244                             *c_end = '\0';
245                             if (!accept_to_eol) execute_a_command();
246                         }
247                     }
248                 break;
249
250                 case F1:                      /* call help file                */
251                     system("help \\rk.hlp");
252                     prompt = TRUE;
```

```
253              break;
254
255              case HOME:                        /* cursor to beginning of line   */
256                  if (current < c_end) {
257                      set_cursor(x_position, y_position);
258                      update_display = FALSE;
259                  }
260                  current = com_buf;
261              break;
262
263              case INS:                         /* cursor forward a word         */
264                  x = (int)(current == c_end);
265                  if (x && (*pred_buf == '\n')) execute_a_command();
266                  else if (current <= c_end) {
267                      ptr = (x) ? pred_buf : current;
268                                                 /* accept any leading non-alpha  */
269                      while (*ptr && !(isalnum(*ptr)) && (*ptr != '\n'))
270                          *current++ = *ptr++;
271                                                 /* ... then the word             */
272                      while (*ptr && isalnum(*ptr))
273                          *current++ = *ptr++;
274                                                 /* ... finally trailing spaces   */
275                      while (*ptr && isspace(*ptr) && (*ptr != '\n'))
276                          *current++ = *ptr++;
277
278                      if (x) {
279                          c_end = current;
280                          *c_end = '\0';
281                      }
282                  }
283              break;
284
285              case PgUp:                        /* previous prediction           */
286                  if (pred_number) pred_number--;
287                  else putchar(BELL);
288              break;
289
290              case PgDn:                        /* next prediction               */
291                  if (++pred_number > (MAX_SET - 1)) {
292                      pred_number--;
293                      putchar(BELL);
294                  }
295              break;
296
297              default:  putchar(BELL);          /* unknown function key code     */
298              break;
299
300              }                                 /* end of inner switch           */
301          break;                                /* done all the function keys    */
302
303          /* finally, handle visible ASCII characters                           */
304
305          default:                              /* add new char at current posn  */
306              if (current == c_end) {           /* at end of line?               */
307                  *current++ = c;
308                  c_end = current;
309                  *c_end = '\0';
310              }
311              else {                            /* within the line               */
312                  for(ptr = c_end++; ptr >= current; ptr--) *(ptr + 1) = *ptr;
313                  *current++ = c;
314              }
315          break;
316
317          }                                     /* end of outer switch           */
318      }                                         /* end of while (1)              */
```

```
318    }
319
320
321    /* DISPLAY COMMAND AND PREDICTION                                           */
322
323    static display_line(displaying)
324    char displaying;
325    {
326        register   int     position,            /* current character position   */
327                           end_length,          /* length of last part of line  */
328                           total_length;        /* total length of displayed line */
329                   char    c,                   /* generic character            */
330                           * ptr = pred_buf;    /* pointer that scans prediction */
331                   int     x1, y1, x2, y2;      /* screen coordinates           */
332
333        set_cursor(x_position, y_position);     /* first part of the command ... */
334        c = *current;
335        *current = '\0';
336        Printf("%s", com_buf);                  /* ... up to current cursor posn */
337
338        get_cursor(&x1, &y1);
339        total_length = strlen(com_buf);
340        *current = c;
341        end_length = strlen(current);
342        Printf("%s", current);                  /* ... from current cursor onward */
343
344        if (displaying) {                       /* now the prediction part      */
345            while (*ptr && *ptr != '\n') ptr++;
346            if (*ptr == '\n') {                 /* ... temporarily replace \n   */
347                *ptr = '\0';
348                c = TRUE;
349            }
350            else c = FALSE;
351                                                /* show pred in inverse video   */
352            invon();
353            Printf("%s%s", pred_buf, (c) ? "^M" : "" );
354            invoff();
355            if (c) *ptr = '\n';
356            end_length += strlen(pred_buf);
357        }
358
359        get_cursor(&x2, &y2);                   /* finally update cursor position */
360        clear_to_end(x2, y2);
361        position = y1 + (end_length + x1) / 80;
362        if (position > 25) y1 -= (position - 25);
363        set_cursor(x1, y1);
364        total_length += end_length;
365        position = y_position + (total_length + x_position) / 80;
366        if (position > 25) y_position -= (position - 25);
367    }
368
369
370    /* SEND A COMMAND LINE TO DOS                                                */
371
372    static execute_a_command()
373    {
374        display_line(FALSE);                     /* update the display ...       */
375        if (*com_buf) {                          /* something on the line?       */
376            putchar('\n');
377            system(com_buf);                     /* ... execute the command ...  */
378        }
379        *c_end++ = '\n';                         /* ... temporarily append a \n  */
380        *c_end-- = '\0';
381        update_the_model(com_buf);               /* ... and update the model     */
382        *c_end = '\0';
383
```

```
384        if (++last_command == MAX_HIST) last_command = 0;
385        if (strlen(com_buf) > MAX_SAVE)          /* save the command in history   */
386            strncpy(prev_buf[last_command], com_buf, MAX_SAVE);
387        else strcpy(prev_buf[last_command], com_buf);
388        t_last_command = last_command;
389        current = c_end = com_buf;                /* reinitialize pointers         */
390        *c_end = '\0';
391        prompt = TRUE;
392    }


393    /*  CLEAR LINE TO END OF DISPLAY (BIOS video function call)                    */
394
395    clear_to_end(x, y)
396    int x, y;
397    {
398        union REGS regs;
399
400        regs.h.ah = 9;
401        regs.h.al = 32;
402        regs.h.bh = 0;
403        regs.h.bl = 7;
404        regs.h.cl = 80 * 24 - y * 24 - x;
405        int86(0x10, &regs, &regs);
406    }


409    /*  GET CURSOR LOCATION (BIOS video function call)                             */
410
411    get_cursor(x, y)
412    int * x, * y;
413    {
414        union REGS regs;
415
416        regs.h.ah = 3;
417        regs.h.bh = 0;
418        int86(0X10, &regs, &regs);
419        *x = regs.h.dl + 1;
420        *y = regs.h.dh + 1;
421    }


424    /*  SET CURSOR LOCATION (BIOS video function call)                             */
425
426    set_cursor(x, y)
427    int x, y;
428    {
429        union REGS regs;
430
431        regs.h.ah = 2;
432        regs.h.dh = y - 1;
433        regs.h.dl = x - 1;
434        regs.h.bh = 0;
435        int86(0X10, &regs, &regs);
436    }
```

```
437     /*************************************************************************
438     *                                                                       *
439     *    rk_pred.c -- Predictive text generator for the Reactive Keyboard   *
440     *                                                                       *
441     *    external interfaces:                                               *
442     *        construct_the_model()                                          *
443     *        make_a_prediction(command, prediction, number)                 *
444     *            char * command, * prediction; int * number                 *
445     *        update_the_model(command_line)  char * command                 *
446     *        prime_from_file()                                              *
447     *        read_setup()                                                   *
448     *                                                                       *
449     *************************************************************************/
450
451     #include <stdio.h>
452     #include <errno.h>
453
454     #define MAX_K       10                  /* maximum order of the model    */
455     #define MAX_FNAME   50                  /* maximum size of a filename    */
456     #define MAX_SET     128                 /* maximum number of symbols     */
457     #define MAX_BUF     256                 /* maximum size of a text buffer */
458
459     /* if the ANSI display driver (ansi.sys) is installed, use it           */
460
461     #ifdef ansi
462         #define invon()     printf("\033[7m") /* ansi inverse on            */
463         #define invoff()    printf("\033[m")  /* ansi inverse off           */
464         #define clear_line() printf("\033[K") /* clear to end of line       */
465         #define Printf      printf
466     #else
467         #define invon()     textattr(0x70)   /* inverse video on            */
468         #define invoff()    textattr(0x07)   /* inverse video off           */
469         #define clear_line() clreol()        /* clear to end of line        */
470         #define Printf      cprintf
471     #endif
472
473     /* global type definitions                                             */
474
475     typedef struct node {                   /* variable-length tree node     */
476         char        the_character;          /* ASCII symbol value            */
477         char        count;                  /* frequency count (to max_freq) */
478         struct node * next;                 /* next predictions at this level */
479         struct node * down;                 /* next level down in the tree   */
480     } Node;
481     typedef Node    * NodePtr;              /* a pointer to a tree node      */
482     typedef NodePtr   TreePtr[MAX_K + 1];   /* k pointers into the tree      */
483
484     /* various setup parameters normally reset using the SETUP utility      */
485
486     static char    prime_file[MAX_FNAME]    /* file to prime from            */
487                         = "\\rk\\rk.prm",
488                    log_file[MAX_FNAME]       /* file to log into             */
489                         = "\\rk\\rk.prm",
490                    zero_freq_file[MAX_FNAME] /* if not found use default above */
491                         = "\\rk\\rk.zff";
492
493     static int     max_len  = 30,           /* prediction length             */
494                    max_k    = 8,             /* model length                  */
495                    max_freq = 127,           /* maximum frequency for node    */
496                    max_nodes = 8 * 1024,     /* initial size of free_nodes[]  */
497                    max_prime = 4 * 1024;     /* maximum characters to prime   */
498
499     /* the following display parameters are also used by main() in rk_com.c  */
500
501         char    accept_to_eol = 0,          /* exclude nl from accept to eol? */
502                 pred_mode     = 1,          /* show predictions              */
```

```
503                    display_prompt = 1;           /* show prompt                   */

504     /* global variables                                                          */
505
506     static char zero_freq[MAX_SET] = {           /* zero frequency table          */
507
508                     '\n',     ' ',     'e',     's',     't',     'r',     'a',     'l',
509                     'n',      '.',     'c',     'i',     'm',     'o',     'd',     'h',
510                     'p',      'u',     'f',     'b',     'w',     'g',     '-',     'y',
511                     '/',      'v',     'k',     '*',     'x',     '5',     '1',     '2',
512                     '4',      '>',     'q',     '\07',   '3',     'z',     '0',     'j',
513                     'M',      'I',     '6',     '\'',    'E',     '~',     'A',     ',',
514                     'S',      'D',     'R',     '?',     'C',     '|',     'B',     'T',
515                     'P',      'U',     '!',     '_',     '<',     'N',     '8',     '@',
516                     '&',      '7',     '\\',    '"',     'J',     ')',     '(',     '[',
517                     ']',      'F',     'L',     ':',     'O',     'K',     '9',     'H',
518                     '+',      '$',     'W',     'Y',     '=',     'G',     ';',     '^',
519                     '{',      'X',     'Q',     '#',     '}',     'V',     '%',     'Z',
520                     '`',      '\b',    '\t',    '\26',   '\00',   '\01',   '\02',   '\03',
521                     '\04',    '\05',   '\06',   '\13',   '\f',    '\r',    '\16',   '\17',
522                     '\20',    '\21',   '\22',   '\23',   '\24',   '\25',   '\27',   '\30',
523                     '\31',    '\32',   '\33',   '\34',   '\35',   '\36',   '\37',   '\177'};
524
525     static NodePtr    free_nodes,             /* array of free nodes           */
526                       root,                   /* the root of the model         */
527                       create_node(), find_char(), insert_char();
528
529     static TreePtr    last_pointer,           /* k pointers into the tree      */
530                       curr_pointer;           /* current pointers into the tree */
531
532     static char       first[MAX_SET],         /* first letter of predictions   */
533                       curr_context[MAX_BUF],  /* current context, string buffer */
534                       prev_context[MAX_K + 1], /* to remember previous contexts */
535                       last_chars[MAX_K + 1],  /* last max_k chars put in model  */
536                       best_pred();
537
538
539     /*   INITIALIZE AND PRIME THE MODEL                                          */
540
541     construct_the_model()
542     {
543         register  int    i;                   /* array index and tree level    */
544                   char   c;                   /* input character               */
545                   FILE   * from;              /* file to read from             */
546                   void   * malloc();          /* system memory allocator       */
547
548         free_nodes = (NodePtr) malloc((unsigned) (max_nodes * sizeof(Node)));
549
550         if (free_nodes == NULL) {             /* exit if not enough memory     */
551             fprintf(stderr, "\n\nRK ran out of memory: %d nodes ", max_nodes);
552             fprintf(stderr, "require %ld bytes.\n", max_nodes * sizeof(Node));
553             fprintf(stderr, "Use the SETUP program to reduce \"max_nodes\" ");
554             fprintf(stderr, "then restart RK.\nExiting RK.\n");
555             exit(1);
556         }
557         else {                                /* create and prime the model    */
558
559             root = create_node();             /* set up root and tree pointers */
560             *curr_pointer = *last_pointer = root;
561             root->down = root->next = NULL;
562             root->count = 1;
563             for (i = 1; i <= max_k; i++) curr_pointer[i] = last_pointer[i] = NULL;
564                                               /* read zero frequency file?     */
565             if ((from = fopen(zero_freq_file, "r")) != NULL) {
566                 i = 0;
```

```
567                    while ((((int)(c = getc(from))) != EOF) {
568                         zero_freq[i++] = c;
569                         if ((((int)(c = getc(from))) == EOF) break;
570                         if (i > 127) break;
571                    }
572               }
573                                                     /* if user has prime file, use it */
574           if ((from = fopen(prime_file, "r+")) != NULL) {
575               prime(from, last_pointer);
576               for (i = 1; i <= max_k; i++) curr_pointer[i] = last_pointer[i];
577               fseek(from, -(max_k + 1), 2);    /* save last chars for context    */
578               for (i = 0; i < max_k; i++) {
579                    if ((((int)(c = getc(from))) == EOF) break;
580                    else last_chars[i] = prev_context[i] = c;
581               }
582               last_chars[i] = prev_context[i] = '\0';
583               fclose(from);
584               find_first_chars(last_pointer); /* prepare initial predictions     */
585           }
586      }
587  }
588
589
590  /*  PRIME THE MODEL                                                             */
591
592  static prime(from, tree_pointer)
593  FILE     * from;
594  TreePtr     tree_pointer;
595  {
596      register    int     level,           /* level of the tree                */  */
597                          size;            /* amount to prime                  */  */
598                  char    c;               /* input character                  */  */
599
600      fseek(from, 0L, 2);                  /* how long is the file?            */  */
601      size = ftell(from);
602      if (size > max_prime) {
603           size = max_prime;
604           fseek(from, -size, 2);           /* set read ptr to correct spot     */  */
605      }
606      else rewind(from);
607
608      Printf("\nPriming from file: %s: ", prime_file);
609      show_progress(size);                 /* actually do the priming          */  */
610      while ((((int)(c = getc(from))) != EOF) {
611           for (level = max_k; level > 0; level--)
612                tree_pointer[level] = insert_char(tree_pointer[level - 1], c);
613           if ((size-- % 100) == 0) show_progress(size + 1);
614      }
615      show_progress(-1);                   /* report that priming is done      */  */
616  }
617
618
619  /*  INSERT CURRENT CHARACTER INTO MODEL IN CONTEXT K DOWN TO 1                 */
620
621  static NodePtr insert_char(current_level_pointer, the_character)
622  NodePtr     current_level_pointer;
623  char        the_character;
624  {
625      NodePtr     start_ptr,               /* start of the predictions         */  */
626                  nptr,                    /* current node pointer             */  */
627                  prev_nptr = NULL,        /* previous node pointer above      */  */
628                  fptr,                    /* for resorting by freq count      */  */
629                  prev_fptr = NULL;        /* previous node pointer above      */  */
630      enum {START,SCANNING,FOUND,END} state;  /* state of the search           */  */
631
```

```
632        if (current_level_pointer == NULL)      /* no sub-tree at this level    */
633            nptr = NULL;
634        else {                                   /* scan for the character ...   */
635
636            if ((start_ptr = current_level_pointer->down) == NULL)
637                state = START;                   /* new character -- first in list */
638            else {
639                                                  /* scan along the linked list ... */
640                fptr = nptr = start_ptr;
641                state = SCANNING;
642                do {                              /* ... to find the character    */
643
644                    if (nptr == NULL)             /* new character -- last in list */
645                        state = END;
646                    else {                        /* ... carry on scanning        */
647                                                  /* ... in correct freq order?   */
648                        if (fptr->count > nptr->count) {
649                            fptr = nptr;          /* ... save for possible swap   */
650                            prev_fptr = prev_nptr;
651                        }
652                        if (nptr->the_character == the_character)
653                            state = FOUND;        /* old character -- found in list */
654                        else {
655                                                  /* ... remember node and continue */
656                            prev_nptr = nptr;
657                            nptr = nptr->next;
658                        }
659                    }                             /* end of if nptr == NULL       */
660                } while (state == SCANNING);
661            }                                     /* end of if start_ptr == NULL  */
662
663            switch (state) {
664
665            case FOUND:                           /* is this node out of order?   */
666                if (fptr != nptr) {               /* ie. fptr->count <= nptr->count */
667                    if (prev_fptr == NULL)        /* ... swap pointers saved above */
668                        current_level_pointer->down = nptr;
669                    else prev_fptr->next = nptr;
670                    prev_nptr->next = nptr->next;
671                    nptr->next = fptr;
672                }                                 /* increment count of the char  */
673                if (++(nptr->count) ==            /* is count about to overflow?  */
674                    max_freq) {                   /* halve all counts at this level */
675                    while (start_ptr != NULL) {
676                        start_ptr->count++;       /* increment (to keep them > 0) */
677                        start_ptr->count >>= 1;   /* ... and halve by shifting    */
678                        start_ptr = start_ptr->next;
679                    }
680                }
681            break;
682
683            case START:                           /* add a new node at this level */
684            case END:
685                nptr = create_node();
686                nptr->the_character               /* ... fill in the prediction,  */
687                    = the_character;
688                nptr->count = 1;                  /* ... the initial count,       */
689                nptr->down = nptr->next = NULL;   /* ... and the associated ptrs  */
690                if (state == START) current_level_pointer->down = nptr;
691                else prev_nptr->next = nptr;
692            break;
693            }                                     /* end of switch                */
694        }                                         /* end of if current_level_ptr  */
695        return(nptr);
696    }
697
```

```
698
699    /*  RETURN A POINTER TO A NEW NODE                                            */
700
701    static NodePtr create_node()
702    {
703        static int     next_free = 0;            /* index to the free node list   */
704               NodePtr nptr;                     /* current node pointer          */
705               void    * malloc();               /* system memory allocator       */
706
707        if (next_free < max_nodes)               /* get a node from the heap      */
708            nptr = &free_nodes[next_free];
709        else {                                   /* if empty, create a new node   */
710            nptr = (NodePtr) malloc((unsigned) sizeof(Node));
711            if (nptr == NULL) {                  /* out of memory?                */
712                fprintf(stderr, "\n\nRK ran out of memory: %d nodes;", next_free);
713                fprintf(stderr, " %ld bytes.\n", next_free * sizeof(Node));
714                fprintf(stderr, "Use the SETUP program to reduce \"max_nodes\",");
715                fprintf(stderr, " then restart RK.\nExiting RK.\n");
716                exit(1);
717            }
718        }
719        next_free++;
720        return(nptr);
721    }
722
723
724    /*  PRINT A NUMBER TO INDICATE PROGRESS WHEN PRIMING                           */
725
726    static show_progress(counter)
727    int counter;
728    {
729        int    x, y;                             /* current screen position       */
730
731        get_cursor(&x, &y);
732        clear_to_end(x, y);
733        if (counter >= 0) {
734            invon();
735            Printf(" %4d ", counter);
736            invoff();
737        }
738        else Printf(" Done");
739        set_cursor(x, y);
740    }
741
742
743    /*  RETURN POINTER TO THE CURRENT PREDICTION                                   */
744
745    make_a_prediction(command, prediction, number)
746    char    * command, * prediction;
747    int     * number;
748    {
749        register   int i;                        /* string length and tree level  */
750                   char * ptr = curr_context;    /* context string pointer        */
751
752        strcpy(curr_context, last_chars);        /* find current context          */
753        strcat(curr_context, command);           /* ensure context length <= max_k */
754        if ((i = strlen(curr_context)) > max_k) ptr = &curr_context[i - max_k];
755
756        if (strcmp(prev_context, ptr)) {         /* context changed from previous? */
757            strcpy(prev_context, ptr);           /* save the new context          */
758            *number = 0;
759            for (i = 1; i <= max_k; i++) curr_pointer[i] = NULL;
760            while (*ptr) {                       /* initialize current tree ptrs  */
761                for (i = max_k; i > 0; i--)
762                    curr_pointer[i] = find_char(curr_pointer[i - 1], *ptr);
763                ptr++;
```

```
764                    }
765                    find_first_chars(curr_pointer);     /* prepare initial predictions    */
766               }
767          else strcpy(prev_context, ptr);          /* complete current prediction    */
768          extend_pred(curr_pointer, prediction, *number);
769     }
770
771
772     /*  FIND FIRST CHARACTERS OF ALL PREDICTIONS IN CONTEXT                        */
773
774     static find_first_chars(tree_pointer)
775     TreePtr     tree_pointer;
776     {
777          static     char     pred_set[MAX_SET];     /* flags chars already on first[] */
778                     char   * ptr;                    /* pred_set and zero_freq ptr     */
779          register   int      level,                 /* current level in tree          */
780                              index = 0;              /* indexes into first[]           */
781                     NodePtr nptr;                    /* current node pointer           */
782
783          for (ptr = pred_set; ptr < &pred_set[MAX_SET]; ptr++) *ptr = '\0';
784
785          for (level = max_k - 1; level >= 0; level--) {
786              if (tree_pointer[level] != NULL)
787                  if (tree_pointer[level]->down != NULL) {
788                      nptr = tree_pointer[level]->down;
789                      while (nptr != NULL) {        /* add unique preds to first[] ...*/
790                          if (!pred_set[(int)nptr->the_character]) {
791                              pred_set[(int)nptr->the_character]++;
792                              first[index++] = nptr->the_character;
793                          }
794                          nptr = nptr->next;        /* scanning current level of tree */
795                      }
796                  }
797          }                                         /* append zero-frequency chars    */
798          for (ptr = zero_freq; ptr < &zero_freq[MAX_SET]; ptr++)
799              if (!pred_set[(int)*ptr]) first[index++] = *ptr;
800     }
801
802
803     /*  EXTEND A PREDICTION, GIVEN ITS INITIAL CHARACTER                           */
804
805     static extend_pred(tree_pointer, prediction, number)
806     TreePtr     tree_pointer;
807     char      * prediction;
808     int         number;
809     {
810          register   int      level,                 /* current level in tree          */
811                              len;                    /* prediction length              */
812                     char   c,                        /* predicted character            */
813                            * ptr = prediction;       /* pointer to growing prediction  */
814                     TreePtr t;                       /* k pointers into the tree       */
815
816          c = first[number];                         /* start with the first char      */
817          for (level = 0; level <= max_k; level++) t[level] = tree_pointer[level];
818          for (len = 0; len < max_len; len++) {   /* adjust pointers to new context */
819              *ptr++ = c;                            /* append the predicted character */
820              if (c == '\n') break;                  /* could continue here if desired */
821              for (level = max_k; level >= 1; level--)
822                  t[level] = find_char(t[level - 1], c);
823              c = best_pred(t);                      /* extend the prediction          */
824          }
825          *ptr = '\0';
826     }
827
828
```

```
829      /*  SCAN THE MODEL FOR PREDICTIONS, RETURNING TREE POINTERS                */
830
831      static NodePtr find_char(current_node_pointer, the_character)
832      NodePtr current_node_pointer;
833      char    the_character;
834      {
835          NodePtr nptr;                           /* current node pointer          */
836
837          if (current_node_pointer == NULL) return(NULL);
838          else {                                  /* scan for the first prediction */
839              nptr = current_node_pointer->down;
840              while (1) {
841                  if (nptr == NULL) return(NULL);
842                  else if (nptr->the_character == the_character) return(nptr);
843                  else nptr = nptr->next;
844              }
845          }
846      }
847
848
849      /*  RETURN THE SINGLE BEST PREDICTION FOR THIS CONTEXT                       */
850
851      static char best_pred(tree_pointer)
852      TreePtr tree_pointer;
853      {
854          register int level = max_k - 1;         /* current level in tree         */
855
856          while (1) {
857              if (tree_pointer[level] != NULL)
858                  if (tree_pointer[level]->down != NULL)
859                      return (tree_pointer[level]->down->the_character);
860              if (level-- == 0) return((char)1);
861          }
862      }
863
864
865      /*  INCORPORATE A COMMAND LINE INTO THE MODEL                                */
866
867      update_the_model(command_line)
868      char * command_line;
869      {
870          register   int i;                       /* string length and tree level  */
871                     char * ptr = command_line;   /* command and context pointer   */
872
873          while (*ptr) {                          /* insert each char into model   */
874              for (i = max_k; i > 0; i--)
875                  last_pointer[i] = insert_char(last_pointer[i - 1], *ptr);
876              ptr++;
877          }
878          log_to_file(command_line);              /* save command for later priming */
879
880          strcpy(curr_context, last_chars);       /* find current context          */
881          strcat(curr_context, command_line);     /* ensure context length <= max_k */
882          if ((i = strlen(curr_context)) > max_k) ptr = &curr_context[i - max_k];
883          else ptr = curr_context;
884
885          strcpy(last_chars, ptr);                /* save last chars added to model */
886      }
887
888
889      /*  SAVE COMPLETED COMMANDS                                                  */
890
891      static log_to_file(command_line)
892      char * command_line;
893      {
```

```
894        FILE    * to,                            /* file to log to              */
895              * fopen();
896
897        if (*command_line != '\n') {            /* do not log blank lines      */
898            if ((to = fopen(log_file, "a")) == NULL) {
899                if (errno == 8) {               /* out of memory?              */
900                    fprintf(stderr, "RK appears to have run out of memory. ");
901                    fprintf(stderr, "Use the SETUP program to reduce \"max_nodes\"");
902                    fprintf(stderr, " or \"max_k\"; then restart RK.\n");
903                }
904                else {
905                    fprintf(stderr, "\nCannot access your log file: %s.", log_file);
906                    fprintf(stderr, "Use the SETUP program to change");
907                    fprintf(stderr, " \"log_file\"; then restart RK.\n");
908                }
909                fprintf(stderr, "Exiting RK.\n");
910                exit(1);
911            }
912            else {                              /* save current command line   */
913                fputs(command_line, to);
914                fflush(to);
915                fclose(to);
916            }
917        }
918    }
919
920
921    /*  PRIME THE MODEL FROM A FILE                                              */
922
923    prime_from_file()
924    {
925        register  int     level;                /* current level in tree       */
926                  FILE    * from;               /* file to prime from          */
927                  TreePtr tree_pointer;         /* k pointers into the tree    */
928
929        clear_line();                           /* prompt for and read file name */
930        Printf("Enter the file name to prime from:\n");
931        gets(curr_context);
932
933        if (!(*curr_context)) Printf("\nCommand cancelled.\n");
934        else if ((from = fopen(curr_context, "r")) == NULL)
935            Printf("\nCannot open %s.\n", curr_context);
936        else {
937            for (level = 0; level <= max_k; level++) tree_pointer[level] = NULL;
938            prime(from, tree_pointer);
939            Printf("\nModel successfully primed from file: %s.\n", curr_context);
940            fclose(from);
941        }
942    }
943
944    /*  READ SETUP PARAMETERS                                                    */
945
946    read_setup()
947    {
948        int     i;                              /* character string lengths    */
949        char    * setup_file;                   /* name of setup file          */
950        FILE    * from;                         /* file pointer to setup file  */
951
952        if (!(setup_file = (char *)searchpath("rk.def"))) setup_file = "rk.def";
953        if ((from = fopen(setup_file, "r")) == NULL) {
954            fprintf(stderr, "\nCannot access your setup file: %s.", setup_file);
955            fprintf(stderr, "Use the SETUP program to create one, then ");
956            fprintf(stderr, "restart RK.\nExiting RK.\n");
957            exit(1);
        }
```

```
958        else {
959            Printf("\n\nReading setup from file:- %s: ", setup_file);
960                    fscanf(from, "%d ", &i);
961            if (i)  fscanf(from, "%s",  prime_file);
962                    fscanf(from, "%d ", &i);
963            if (i)  fscanf(from, "%s",  log_file);
964                    fscanf(from, "%d ", &i);
965            if (i)  fscanf(from, "%s",  zero_freq_file);
966                    fscanf(from, "%d ", & accept_to_eol);
967                    fscanf(from, "%d ", & pred_mode);
968                    fscanf(from, "%d ", & display_prompt);
969                    fscanf(from, "%d ", & max_k);
970                    fscanf(from, "%d ", & max_nodes);
971                    fscanf(from, "%d ", & max_prime);
972                    fscanf(from, "%d ", & max_freq);
973                    fscanf(from, "%d ", & max_len);
974            fclose(from);
975            if (max_freq > 126)                    /* keep char node->count < 128   */
976                max_freq = 126;                    /* see insert_char case: FOUND   */
977            Printf("Done");
978        }
979    }
```

Appendix D

List of Sources

Brown Bag Software
2155 South Bascome Ave., Suite 114
Campbell, CA 95008

Clwyd Technics Ltd.
Antelope Industrial Estate
Rhydymwyn Mold
Clwyd
Wales CH7 5JH

DLM Teaching Resources
One DLM Park
Allen, TX 75002

Microsystems Software, Inc.
600 Worcester Rd.
Framingham, MA 01701

NanoPac, Inc.
4833 South Sheridan Rd., Suite 402
Tulsa, OK 74145-5718

National Support Center for Persons
   with Disabilities
Box 2150
Atlanta, GA 30055

P.C.D. Maltron Ltd.
15 Orchard Lane
East Molsey
Surrey
England KT8 0BN

Pointer Systems, Inc.
One Mill St.
Burlington, VT 05401

Prentke Romich Co.
1022 Heyl Rd.
Wooster, OH 44691

Scetlander Ltd.
74 Victoria Crescent Rd.
Glasgow
Scotland G12 9JN

Trace Research and Development
   Center
S-151 Waisman Center
University of Wisconsin
1500 Highland Ave.
Madison, WI 53705-2280

Words+ Inc.
Box 1229
44421 Tenth St. West, Suite L
Lancaster, CA 93584

World Communications
245 Tonopah Dr.
Fremont, CA 94539

Zygo Industries, Inc.
Box 1008
Portland, OR 97207-1008

References

Andreae, J. H. (1977). *Thinking with the teachable machine.* London: Academic Press.

Andreae, J. H. (1984). Learning with a multiple context. In *Man Machine Studies Group Progress Report, UC-DSE/23,* pp. 17–47. Department of Electrical and Electronic Engineering, University of Canterbury, Christchurch, New Zealand.

Arnott, J. L., and Javed, M. Y. (1990, June). Small text corpora in character disambiguation for reduced typing keyboards. In *Proceedings of the Thirteenth Annual Conference on Rehabilitation Engineering,* pp. 181–182. Washington, DC.

Arnott, J. L., Pickering, J. A., Swiffin, A. L., and Battison, M. (1984, June). An adaptive and predictive communication aid for the disabled exploits the redundancy in natural language. In *Proceedings of the Second International Conference on Rehabilitation Engineering,* pp. 349–350. Ottawa, Ontario.

Baletsa, G. S. (1977, July). Anticipatory communication. Masters Thesis, Engineering, Tufts New England Medical Center, Medford, MA.

Baletsa, G. S., Foulds, R. A., and Crochetiere, W. (1976, November). Design parameters of an intelligent communication device. In *29th Annual Conference on Engineering in Medicine and Biology,* p. 371. Boston, MA.

Bell, T. C., Cleary, J. G., and Witten, I. H. (1990). *Text compression.* Englewood Cliffs, NJ: Prentice Hall.

Bobrow, D. G., Burchfiel, J. D., Murphy, D L., and Tomlinson, R. S. (1972, March). TENEX, a paged time sharing system for the PDP-10. *Communications of the Association for Computing Machinery, 15*(3): 135–143.

Brady, M., Kelso, D. P., Vanderheiden, G. C., and Buehman, D. (1982, August). A data-based approach to character/syllable/word sets. In *Proceedings of the Fifth Annual Conference on Rehabilitation Engineering,* p. 1, Houston, TX.

Brandenburg, S. A., and Vanderheiden, G. C. (Editors). (1987). *Communication, control, and computer access for disabled and elderly individuals.* Boston, MA: College-Hill Press.

Brown, D. N., Grigg, P. J., and Watts, P. (1982, July). A communication interface using a microcomputer for severely handicapped children. In *Proceedings of the IEE Conference on Man–Machine Interaction,* pp. 201–204. Manchester, England.

Brownlow, N. D., Shein, G. F., Treviranus, J., Milner, M., and Parnes, P. (1990, June). Don't manipulate, delegate! In *Proceedings of the Thirteenth Annual Conference on Rehabilitation Engineering,* pp. 153–154. Washington, DC.

Buhr, P., and Holte, R. (1981). Some considerations in the design of communication aids for the severely physically disabled. *Medical and Biological Engineering and Computing, 19:* 725–733.

Carlson, R., Elenius, K. K., Granstrom, B., and Hunnicutt, M. S. (1985). Phonetic and orthographic properties of the basic vocabulary of five European languages. *Speech Transmission Laboratory Quarterly Progress and Status Report, 1:* 63–94. Department of Speech Communication and Music Acoustics, Royal Institute of Technology, Stockholm, Sweden.

Carroll, J. B. (1966). Word-frequency studies and the lognormal distribution. In *Proceedings of the Conference on Language and Language Behavior,* edited by E. M. Zale, pp. 213–235. New York: Appleton-Century-Crofts.

Chapanis, A., Ochsman, R. B., Parrish, R. N., and Weeks, G. D. (1972). Studies in interactive communication modes on the behaviour of teams during cooperative problem solving. *Human Factors, 14:* 487–509.

Charbonneau, J. R. (1982). Interfaces for physically handicapped persons. In *Computers and the Handicapped: Tutorial*, edited by P. J. Nelson, pp. 26–30. National Research Council of Canada, Ottawa.

Chizinsky, K. A. (1990, June). Keyboard access to the Apple Macintosh. In *Proceedings of the Thirteenth Annual Conference on Rehabilitation Engineering*, pp. 253–254. Washington, DC.

Clarkson, T. G., and Poon, P. E. (1982, July). Utilizing eye-position sensing and user-defined vocabularies to enhance the communication rate of non-vocal people with severe physical impairment. In *Proceedings of the IEE Conference on Man–Machine Interaction*, pp. 174–177. Manchester, England.

Cleary, J. G. (1980). An associative and impressible computer. Ph.D. Thesis, University of Canterbury, Christchurch, New Zealand.

Cleary, J. G. (1984, September). Compact hash tables using bidirectional linear probing. *IEEE Trans Computers, C-33*(9): 828–834.

Cleary, J. G., and Darragh, J. J. (1984). A fast compact representation of trees using hash tables. Research Report 83/162/20, Department of Computer Science, University of Calgary, Alberta.

Cleary, J. G., and Witten, I. H. (1984, April). Data compression using adaptive coding and partial string matching. *IEEE Trans Communications, COM-32*(4): 396–402.

Colby, K. M. (1984, Spring). Intelligent speech and memory prostheses. *ACM SIGCAPH Newsletter, 34:* 16–17.

Colby, K. M., Christinaz, D., and Graham, S. (1978). A computer-driven, personal, portable, and intelligent speech prosthesis. *Computers and Biomedical Research, 11:* 337–343.

Colby, K. M., Christinaz, D., Parkinson, R. C., and Tiefemann, M. (1982, May). Predicting word-expressions to increase output rates of speech prostheses used in communication disorders. In *Proceedings of the IEEE International Conference on Acoustics, Speech and Signal Processing*, pp. 751–754. Paris, France.

Cover, T. M., and King, R. C. (1978, July). A convergent gambling estimate of the entropy of English. *IEEE Trans Information Theory, IT-24*(4): 413–421.

Cress, C. J. (1986, June). Bibliography of vocabulary frequency and wordset analysis studies. Research Report, Trace Research and Development Center, University of Wisconsin-Madison, WI.

Damerau, F. J. (1971). Markov models and linguistic theory: an experimental study of a model of English. *Janua Linguarum, 95.*

Damper, R. I. (1984, June). Speech as a medium for interfacing disabled people to aids. In *Proceedings of the Second International Conference on Rehabilitation Engineering*, pp. 450–451. Ottawa, Ontario.

Darragh, J. J. (1988). Adaptive predictive text generation and the Reactive Keyboard. Research Report 88/343/05, Department of Computer Science, University of Calgary, Alberta.

Darragh, J. J., Cleary, J. G., and Witten, I. H. (1991). Bonsai: a compact representation of trees. Research Report 91/447/31, Department of Computer Science, University of Calgary, Alberta.

Darragh, J. J., and Witten, I. H. (1991, April). Adaptive predictive text generation and the Reactive Keyboard. *Interacting with Computers, 3*(1): 27–50.

Darragh, J. J., Witten, I. H., and Cleary, J. G. (1983). Adaptive text compression to enhance a modem. Research Report 83/132/21, Department of Computer Science, University of Calgary, Alberta.

Darragh, J. J., Witten, I. H., and James, M. L. (1990, November). The Reactive Keyboard: a predictive typing aid. *IEEE Computer, 23*(11): 41–49.

Demasco, P., and Foulds, R. (1982, September). A new horizon for non-vocal communication devices. *Byte, 7*(9): 166–182.

Dunn-Rankin, P. (1978, January). The visual characteristics of words. *Scientific American, 238*(1): 122–130.

Durie, N. D. (1983, March). Interfaces – enablers for the disabled. In *First Canadian Congress of Rehabilitation Workshop*, pp. 1–32. Ottawa, Ontario.

Fitts, P. M. (1954). The information capacity of the human motor system in controlling the amplitude of movement. *Journal of Experimental Psychology, 47:* 381–391.

Foley, J. D., and Wallace, V. L. (1974, April). The art of natural graphic man-machine communication. *Proceedings of the Institute of Electrical and Electronic Engineers, 62*(4): 462–471.

Foulds, R. A. (1980). Communication rates for non-speech expression as a function of manual tasks and linguistic constraints. In *Proceedings of the First International Conference on Rehabilitation Engineering*, pp. 83–87. Toronto, Ontario.

Foulds, R. A., Baletsa, B. S., and Crochetiere, W. J. (1975). The effectiveness of language redundancy in non-verbal communication. In *Proceedings of the Conference on Devices and Systems for the Disabled*, pp. 82–86. Philadelphia, PA.

Gaddis, E. L. (1982, November). Proportional computer interface increases speed of non-vocal communication. In *Proceedings of the IEEE Computer Society Workshop on Computing to Aid the Handicapped*, pp. 69–75. Charlottesville, VA.

Gibler, C. D. (1981, June). Linguistic and human performance considerations in the design of an anticipatory communication aid. Ph.D. Thesis, Northwestern University, Evanston, IL.

Gibler, C. D., and Childress, D. S. (1982, November). Language anticipation with a computer based scanning aid. In *Proceedings of the IEEE Computer Society Workshop on Computing to Aid the Handicapped*, pp. 11–15. Charlottesville, VA.

Goodenough-Trepagnier, C., Galdieri, B., Rosen, M. J., and Baker, E. (1984, June). Slow message production rate and receivers' impatience. In *Proceedings of the Second International Conference on Rehabilitation Engineering*, pp. 347–348. Ottawa, Ontario.

Goodenough-Trepagnier, C., and Rosen, M. J. (1982). An analytic framework for optimizing design and selection of nonvocal communication techniques. In *Proceedings of the International Federation of Automatic Control Conference on Control Aspects of Prosthetics and Orthotics*, pp. 63–78. Columbus, OH.

Goodenough-Trepagnier, C., Rosen, M. J., and Demsetz, L. (1982b, October). Determinants of rate in communication-aids for the non-vocal motor handicapped. *In Proceedings of the Human Factors Society*, pp. 172–175. Seattle, WA.

Goodenough-Trepagnier, C., Tarry, E., and Prather, P. (1982a). Derivation of an efficient nonvocal communication system. *Human Factors, 24*(2): 163–172.

Greenberg, S. (1984). User modeling in interactive computer systems. M.Sc. Thesis, Department of Computer Science, University of Calgary, Alberta.

Greenberg, S. (1988). Tool use, re-use, and organization in command-driven interfaces. Ph.D. Thesis, Department of Computer Science, University of Calgary, Alberta.

Gunderson, J., Kelso, D., and Vanderheiden, G. C. (1982, November). A multifunction alternative computer "keyboard" for the physically handicapped using headpointing techniques. In *Proceedings of the IEEE Computer Society Workshop on Computing to Aid the Handicapped*, pp. 77–82. Charlottesville, VA.

Hall, M., Vanderheiden, G. C., and Thompson, C. (1989). ABLEDATA and Hyper-ABLEDATA. *Assistive Technology, 1*(4): 107–111.

Hamann, G. (1990, June). Two switchless selection techniques using a headpointing device for graphical user interfaces. In *Proceedings of the Thirteenth Annual Conference on Rehabilitation Engineering*, pp. 439–440. Washington, DC.

Hansen, W. J. (1971). User engineering principles for interactive systems. *Proceedings of the American Federation for Information Processing Societies Fall Joint Computer Conference, 39:* 523–532.

Heckathorne, C. W., and Childress, D. S. (1982, November). An integrated computer system for anticipatory text generation and device control by individuals with severe motor impairment.

In *Proceedings of the IEEE Computer Society Conference on Computing to Aid the Handi-capped,* pp. 17–23. Charlottesville, VA.

Heckathorne, C. W., and Childress, D. S. (1983, June). Applying anticipatory text selection in a writing aid for people with severe motor impairment. *IEEE Micro, 3*(3): 17–23.

Heckathorne, C. W., Doubler, J. A., and Childress, D. S. (1980, April). Experience with microproces-sor-based aids for disabled people. In *Proceedings of the IEEE Computer Society Workshop on Applications of Personal Computing to Aid the Handicapped,* pp. 53–56. Laurel, MD.

Heckathorne, C. W., Voda, J. A., and Leibowitz, L. J. (1987, December). Design rationale and evaluation of the portable anticipatory communication aid–PACA. *Journal of Augmentative and Alternative Communication, 3*(4): 170–180.

Henle, R. A. (1981, October). Electronic keyboard. In *Proceedings of the Johns Hopkins First National Search for Applications of Personal Computing to Aid the Handicapped,* pp. 146–149. Baltimore, MD: Johns Hopkins University.

Hunnicutt, M. S. (1986). Lexical prediction for a text-to-speech system. In *Communication and handicap: aspects of psychological compensation and technical aids,* edited by E. Hjelmquist and L. G. Nilsson, pp. 253–263. North-Holland: Elsevier Science Publishers B. V.

Hunnicutt, M. S. (1987). Input and output alternatives in word prediction. *Speech Transmission Laboratory Quarterly Progress and Status Report, 2–3:* 15–29. Department of Speech Com-munication and Music Acoustics, Royal Institute of Technology, Stockholm, Sweden.

Hunnicutt, M. S. (1990, October). Word prediction: exploring the use of semantic and syntactic information. In *Proceedings of the Fourth Biennial Conference of the International Society for Augmentative and Alternative Communication.* Stockholm, Sweden.

Jones, R. L. (1981, October). Row/column scanning with a dynamic matrix. In *Proceedings of the Johns Hopkins First National Search for Applications of Personal Computing to Aid the Handicapped,* pp. 6–8. Baltimore, MD: Johns Hopkins University.

Kelso, D. P., and Gunderson, J. (1984, June). Generic keyboard emulator architecture for transparent access to standard software by handicapped individuals. In *Proceedings of the Second Interna-tional Conference on Rehabilitation Engineering,* pp. 50–51. Ottawa, Ontario.

Kelso, D. P., and Vanderheiden, G. C. (1982, August). Ten-branch abbreviation expansion for greater efficiency in augmentative communication systems. In *Proceedings of the Fifth Annual Con-ference on Rehabilitation Engineering,* p. 3. Houston, TX.

Kernighan, B. W., and Ritchie, D. M. (1978). *The C programming language.* Englewood Cliffs, NJ: Prentice Hall.

Kucera, H., and Francis, W. N. (1967). *Computational analysis of present-day American English.* Providence, RI: Brown University Press.

Lazzaro, J. J. (1990, August). Opening doors for the disabled. *Byte, 15*(8): 258–268.

Lee, K. S., and Thomas, D. J. (1990). *Control of computer-based technology for people with physical disabilities: an assessment manual.* Toronto: University of Toronto Press.

Lindsey, J. D. (Editor). (1987). *Computers and exceptional individuals.* Columbus, OH: Merrill Publishing Co.

Magnuson, T., and Hunnicutt, M. S. (1990, October). Measuring the effect of a word processor with prediction. In *Proceedings of the Fourth Biennial Conference of the International Society for Augmentative and Alternative Communication.* Stockholm, Sweden.

Miller, G. A. (1956, March). The magical number seven, plus or minus two: some limits on our capacity for processing information. *Psychological Review, 63*(2): 81–97.

Mooers, C. N. (1966, March). TRAC, a procedure-describing language for the reactive typewriter. *Communications of the Association for Computing Machinery, 9*(3): 215–219.

Morasso, P., Pesno, M., Suetta, G. P., and Tagliasco, V. (1979). Towards standardization of communication and control systems of motor impaired people. *Medical and Biological Engineering, 17:* 481–488.

Myers, W. (1982, February). Personal computers aid the handicapped. *IEEE Micro, 2*(1): 27–40.

Nelson, P. J., Korba, L. W., and Park, G. C. (1984). Evolution of the MOD keyboard system. In *Proceedings of the IEEE Computer Society Third Annual Workshop on Computing to Aid the Handicapped,* pp. 3–10.

Nelson, P. J., Korba, L. W., Park, G. C., and Crabtree, D. (1983, August). The MOD keyboard. *IEEE Micro, 3:* 7–17.

Newell, A. F. (1989). PAL and CHAT: human interfaces for extraordinary situations. In *Computing Technologies, new directions and applications,* edited by P. Salanieks, pp. 103–127. Chichester, England: Ellis Horwood.

Newell, A. F., Booth, L., and Beattie, W. (1991). Predictive text entry with PAL and children with learning difficulties. *British Journal of Educational Technology, 22*(1): 23–40.

Nooteboom, S. G. (1981). Lexical retrieval from fragments of spoken words: beginnings vs endings. *Journal of Phonetics, 9:* 407–424.

Norman, D. A. (1983, April). Design rules based on analysis of human error. *Communications of the Association for Computing Machinery, 26*(4): 254–258.

Perkins, W. H. (1971). *Speech Pathology.* St. Louis, MO: C. V. Mosby Co.

Pickering, J. A., and Stevens, G. C. (1984, June). The physically handicapped and work-related computing: towards interface intelligence. In *Proceedings of the Second International Conference on Rehabilitation Engineering,* pp. 126–127. Ottawa, Ontario.

Pon, B., and Tam, E. (1990, June). The Boss: an alternative direct manipulation file manager for people with physical disabilities. Internal report, Hugh MacMillan Rehabilitation Centre, Microcomputer Applications Programme, Toronto, Ontario.

Pressman, H. (Editor). (1987). *Making an exceptional difference: enhancing the impact of microcomputer technology on children with disabilities.* Boston, MA: Exceptional Parent Press.

Raitzer, G. A., Vanderheiden, G. C., and Holt, C. S. (1976, June). Interfacing computers for the physically handicapped – a review of international approaches. In *Proceedings of the American Federation for Information Processing Societies National Computer Conference,* pp. 209–216. New York, NY.

Rich, E. (1983, March). Users are individuals: individualizing user models. *International Journal of Man–Machine Studies, 18*(3): 199–214.

Ring, N. D. (1980). Communication aids for the speech impaired. In *The use of technology in the care of elderly and the disabled: tools for living,* edited by J. Bray and S. Wright, pp. 79–82. Westport, CT: Greenwood Press.

Ritchie, D. M., and Thompson, K. (1974, July). The UNIX time-sharing system. *Communications of the Association for Computing Machinery, 17*(7): 365–375.

Rogers, B. L., Kelso, D. P., and Vanderheiden, G. C. (1982, August). Design of universal keyboard emulators. In *Proceedings of the Fifth Annual Conference on Rehabilitation Engineering,* p. 45. Houston, TX.

Rosen, M. J., and Goodenough-Trepagnier, C. (1982a, December). Communication systems for the nonvocal handicapped: practice and prospects. *IEEE Engineering in Medicine and Biology Magazine,* pp. 31–35.

Rosen, M. J., and Goodenough-Trepagnier, C. (1982b, August). The influence of scan dimensionality on non-vocal communication rate. In *Proceedings of the Fifth Annual Conference on Rehabilitation Engineering,* p. 4. Houston, TX.

Rosengren, E., and Hunnicutt, M. S. (1990, October). A speech recognition-controlled predicting word processor. In *Proceedings of the Fourth Biennial Conference of the International Society for Augmentative and Alternative Communication.* Stockholm, Sweden.

Salthouse, T. A. (1984, February). The skill of typing. *Scientific American, 250*(2): 128–135.

Schauer, J., Novak, M., Lee, C. C., Vanderheiden, G. C., and Kelso, D. P. (1990, June). Transparent access interface for Apple and IBM computers: the T-TAM. In *Proceedings of the Thirteenth Annual Conference on Rehabilitation Engineering*, pp. 255–256. Washington, DC.

Seibel, R. (1972). Data entry devices and procedures. In *Human Engineering Guide to Equipment Design*, edited by H. VanCott and R. G. Kindale. Washington, DC: American Institute for Research.

Shannon, C. E. (1951, January). Prediction and entropy of printed English. *Bell System Technical J, 30*(1): 50–64.

Shein, G. F. (1988a, June). A prototype expert system for the design of a visual keyboard. In *Proceedings of the International Conference of the Association for the Advancement of Rehabilitation Technology*, pp. 382–383. Montreal, Quebec.

Shein, G. F. (1988b, September). A prototype expert system to customize a visual keyboard as an alternative computer access system for a physically disabled person. In *Proceedings of the Annual Conference of the Human Factors Association of Canada*, pp. 13–16. Edmonton, Alberta.

Shein, G. F., Haataja, S., Brownlow, N. D., Treviranus, J., Milner, M., and Parnes, P. (1990, June). Direct manipulation of text by scanning. In *Proceedings of the Thirteenth Annual Conference on Rehabilitation Engineering*, pp. 147–148. Washington, DC.

Shein, G. F., McDougall, J., Knysh, B., Sainai, D., Lee, K., Brownlow, N. D., and Milner, M. (1989, June). A model for alternative access systems. In *Proceedings of the Twelfth Annual Conference on Rehabilitation Engineering*, pp. 17–18. New Orleans, LA.

Shein, G. F., Treviranus, J., Brownlow, N. D., Milner, M., and Parnes, P. (in press). Human-computer interaction for people with physical disabilities. *International Journal of Industrial Ergonomics*.

Shipley, A. D. C. (1980). Problems in the provision of communication aids. In *The use of technology in the care of elderly and the disabled: tools for living*, edited by J. Bray, and S. Wright, pp. 71–78. Westport, CT: Greenwood Press.

Soede, M., and Foulds, R. A. (1986). Dilemma of prediction in communication aids and mental load. In *Proceedings of the Ninth Annual Conference on Rehabilitation Engineering*, pp. 357–359. Minneapolis, MN.

Staisey, N. L., Tombaugh, J. W., and Dillon, R. F. (1982, July). Videotext and the disabled. *International Journal of Man–Machine Studies, 17*(1): 35–50.

Stallman, R. M. (1981). EMACS – The extensible, customizable, self-documenting display editor. *SIGOA Newsletter, 2*(1/2): 147–156. (*Proceedings of the Association for Computing Machinery Symposium on Text Manipulation*, Portland, OR.)

Standish, T. A. (1980). *Data structure techniques*. Reading, MA: Addison-Wesley.

Stevens, G., Bell, D. W., and Bernstein, J. (1984, June). Telephone communication between deaf and hearing persons using speech-to-text and text-to-speech conversion. In *Proceedings of the Second International Conference on Rehabilitation Engineering*, pp. 273–274. Ottawa, Ontario.

Suen, C. Y. (1979, April). n-gram statistics for natural language understanding and text processing. *IEEE Trans Pattern Analysis and Machine Intelligence, PAMI-1*(2): 164–172.

Swiffen, A. L., Arnott, J. L., and Newell, A. F. (1987a, June). The use of syntax in a predictive communication aid for the physically handicapped. In *Proceedings of the Tenth Annual Conference on Rehabilitation Engineering*, pp. 127–129. San Jose, CA.

Swiffin, A. L., Arnott, J. L., Pickering, J. A., and Newell, A. F. (1987b, December). Adaptive and predictive techniques in a communication prosthesis. *Journal of Augmentative and Alternative Communication, 3*(4): 181–191.

Thimbleby, H. W. (1980, October). Dialogue determination. *International Journal of Man–Machine Studies, 13*(3): 295–304.

Thimbleby, H. W. (1990). *User interface design*. Wokingham, England: Addison-Wesley.

Thomas, A. (1980, September). Devices for the disabled: personal, portable, and affordable. In *Proceedings of the IEEE Computer Society Workshop on Applications of Personal Computing to Aid the Handicapped*, pp. 51–52. Laurel, MD.

Thomas, A. (1981, January). Communication devices for the non-vocal disabled. *IEEE Computer, 14*(1): 25–30.

Vanderheiden, G. C. (1981, January). Practical application of microcomputers to aid the handicapped. *IEEE Computer, 14*(1): 54–61.

Vanderheiden, G. C. (1982, September). Computers can play a dual role for disabled individuals. *Byte, 7*(9): 136–162.

Vanderheiden, G. C. (1983, Summer). Non-conversational communication technology needs of individuals with physical handicaps. *Rehabilitation World, 7*(2).

Vanderheiden, G. C. (1984, June). A high-efficiency flexible keyboard input acceleration technique: speedkey. In *Proceedings of the Second International Conference on Rehabilitation Engineering*, pp. 353–354. Ottawa, Ontario.

Vanderheiden, G. C., and Grilley, K. (1976). *Non-vocal communication techniques and aids for the physically handicapped*. Baltimore: University Park Press.

Vanderheiden, G. C., and Kelso, D. P. (1982, August). Dual and nested computer approach to vocational and educational computer systems. In *Proceedings of the Fifth Annual Conference on Rehabilitation Engineering*, p. 46. Houston, TX.

Vanderheiden, G. C., and Kelso, D. P (1987, December). Comparative analysis of fixed vocabulary communication acceleration techniques. *Journal of Augmentative and Alternative Communication, 3*(4): 196–206.

Weeks, G. D., Kelly, M., and Chapanis, A. (1974). Studies in interactive communication V. Cooperative problem solving by skilled and unskilled typists in a teletypewriter mode. *Journal of Applied Psychology, 59:* 665–674.

Whiteside, J., Archer, N., Wixon, D., and Good, M. (1982, June). How do people really use text editors? In *Proceedings of the ACM SIGOA Conference on Office Information Systems*, pp. 29–40. Philadelphia, PA.

Witten, I. H. (1979, January). Approximate, non-deterministic modelling of behaviour sequences. *International Journal of General Systems, 5:* 1–12.

Witten, I. H. (1981a, January). Some recent results in non-deterministic modelling of behaviour sequences. In *Proceedings of the Society for General Systems Research Annual Conference*, pp. 265–274. Toronto, Ontario.

Witten, I. H. (1981b, June). Programming by example for the casual user: a case study. In *Proceedings of the Canadian Man–Computer Communication Conference*, pp. 105–113. Waterloo, Ontario.

Witten, I. H. (1982, July). An interactive computer terminal interface which predicts user entries. In *Proceedings of the IEE Conference on Man–Machine Interaction*, pp. 1–5. Manchester, England.

Witten, I. H., Cleary, J. G., and Darragh, J. J. (1983, May). The reactive keyboard: a new technology for text entry. In *Proceedings of the Canadian Information Processing Society Conference*, pp. 151–156. Ottawa, Ontario.

Witten, I. H., Cleary, J. G., Darragh, J. J., and Hill, D. R. (1982, November). Reducing keystroke counts with a predictive computer interface. In *Proceedings of the IEEE Computer Society Conference on Computing to Aid the Handicapped*, pp. 3–10. Charlottesville, VA.

Yang, G., McCoy, K., and Demasco. P. (1990, June). Word prediction using a semantic tree adjoining grammar. In *Proceedings of the Thirteenth Annual Conference on Rehabilitation Engineering*, pp. 185–186. Washington, DC.

Young, C. (1981, October). Versa-scan keyboardless input system for personal computer use by severely disabled persons. In *Proceedings of the Johns Hopkins First National Search for Applications of Personal Computing to Aid the Handicapped*, pp. 193–195. Baltimore, MD: Johns Hopkins University.

Index